Praise for

FROM BAPTIST PREACHER
TO MORMON TEACHER

"Truth is truth, and for most people it doesn't always come in a pretty package. Wain shares the truth and insights about why he believes what he believes. *From Baptist Preacher to Mormon Teacher* is not for the weak of heart! Wain Myers is taking no prisoners as he shares his raw, yet personal, experience of leaving the 'cloth' and embracing the priesthood. His real, refreshing testimony will uplift you and remind you that, like the scriptures say, we are more than a conqueror!"

—Tamu Smith and Zandra Vranes, authors of
SISTASinZION.com and *Diary of Two Mad Black Mormons*

"*From Baptist Preacher to Mormon Teacher* is a quick and delightful read. Full of compelling insights, it is also humorous, instructive, and thought-provoking. Readers will not only feel edified by reading this book, but they will feel like they've gained a new, wise, and very funny friend."

—Margaret Young, author and filmmaker

"An inspirational story of trials and triumphs with a moving portrayal about confronting the issues surrounding African Americans and the priesthood. Don't miss it!"

—Kimball Fisher, author of *The Christlike Leader*

"As one fingerprint can have certain similarities to another, when looking at the entire print, each becomes unique. The same is true for conversions to the Church. Certain aspects of the conversion may be similar to another convert, but when viewing the entire experience, each is distinctive. Brother Wain Myers is no exception. The uniqueness of his story is compelling and faith promoting but, like the Prophet Joseph, becomes profoundly similar when personal revelation flooded Brother Myers's soul that none of the churches, other than the one that Heavenly Father would set his course on, was the Lord's true Church. Clothed in faith, the Reverend Wain Myers begins the search."

—Dan Barker, author of *Seeds of Faith*

"Wain Myers has a unique way of telling his story that is conversational and delivers two books for the price of one. He gets personal as he shares his own background as a Baptist preacher and also assumes the role as a Mormon teacher. Going back and forth between the two, readers are given a fascinating perspective because of his understanding of both religions, while getting to know Wain at the same time as a powerful instrument in the hands of God."

—Selena Pannell, coauthor of *3,000 Miles to Eternity*

"When confronted with a fact that hurt him to his very core, rather than take the position of a man indignant, Wain laid aside the thing that offended him in favor of trusting that God was answering his prayer in His own way and time. He might have left the Church and never looked back, but Brother Myers has such a relationship with his Heavenly Father that he endured the pain for a greater good. This compelling response stands in stark contrast to the world that we live in today."

—Duane Pannell, coauthor of *3,000 Miles to Eternity*

FROM BAPTIST PREACHER TO MORMON TEACHER

FROM BAPTIST PREACHER TO MORMON TEACHER

WAIN MYERS

with KELLY L. MARTINEZ

CFI
An Imprint of Cedar Fort, Inc.
Springville, UT

ISBN 13: 978-1-4621-1702-4

Published by CFI, an imprint of Cedar Fort, Inc.
2373 W. 700 S., Springville, UT 84663
Distributed by Cedar Fort, Inc., www.cedarfort.com

LIBRARY OF CONGRESS CATALOGING-IN-PUBLICATION DATA

Myers, Wain, 1969- author.
From Baptist preacher to Mormon teacher / Wain Myers with Kelly L. Martinez.
    pages cm
Summary: Life story and experiences of black Mormon convert Wain Myers.
Includes bibliographical references.
ISBN 978-1-4621-1702-4 (perfect bound : alk. paper)
1. Myers, Wain, 1969- 2. Mormon converts--Biography. 3. African American Mormons--Biography. I. Martinez, Kelly L., 1967- author. II. Title.

BX8695.M94A3 2015
289.3092--dc23
[B]

2015022014

Cover design by Shawnda T. Craig
Cover design © 2015 Lyle Mortimer
Edited and typeset by Jessica B. Ellingson

Printed in the United States of America

10 9 8 7 6 5 4 3 2 1

Printed on acid-free paper

For our Heavenly Father, who brought us together to work on this book.

W. M. and K. L. M.

CONTENTS

Preface 1

SECTION I: From Baptist Preacher

Chapter 1: From Student to Teacher 5

Chapter 2: My Joseph Smith Experience 15

Chapter 3: The Wrong Path 21

Chapter 4: The Love Bus 27

Chapter 5: Sebrina's Story 31

Chapter 6: The White Guys with the Name Tags 35

SECTION II: To Mormon Teacher

Chapter 7: A New Beginning 51

Chapter 8: God Is Calling 57

Chapter 9: Patriarchal Blessing 63

Chapter 10: When the Honeymoon Is Over 65

Chapter 11: Wolves in Sheep's Clothing 73

Chapter 12: Blacks and the Priesthood 81

Chapter 13: Testimony and Testifying 85

Chapter 14: Like a Fire Is Burning 93

Chapter 15: Love under New Management 99

Chapter 16: Do You Hear Yo Mama Callin' You? 107

Chapter 17: Keepin' It Real 113

Contents

Chapter 18: Let There Be Light...117

Chapter 19: Called to Serve 123

Chapter 20: Steadfast and Firm 129

About Wain Myers 133

About Kelly L. Martinez.. 134

PREFACE

IN MANY PARTS of the United States, The Church of Jesus Christ of Latter-day Saints' membership comprises mostly white people. That's not the case in other parts of the world, but this book is not about other parts of the world. It's about how a black man in his twenties came to accept the teachings of the LDS Church in the United States, where, based on his experience, the overwhelming majority of Church membership is white. This story tells of the struggles and triumphs of Wain Myers, who in retrospect recognizes that his path to the Church started when he was an eight-year-old boy living in Ohio. That path was filled with obstacles and detours, including a stint serving in the United States Army, the challenge of caring for a mentally ill mother, and years of preaching in the Baptist church.

In essence, this book is about how a Baptist preacher became a Mormon teacher, hence the title.

In spite of his struggles prior to and after joining the LDS Church, Wain's unconquerable spirit and firm belief that the Church is true have provided him with opportunities to reach others *because* of the color of his skin and *because* of his unique perspective as a black man worshipping in the LDS Church.

Sebrina, Wain's wife, has played an important role in this journey. She joined the Church before he did and was an influence for good while he was investigating the Church—and has been ever since. Her story is also worthy of a book, but for now, Wain's story will have to do. You will, however, get a small peek at her story within the pages that follow.

FROM BAPTIST PREACHER TO MORMON TEACHER

How *From Baptist Preacher to Mormon Teacher* came to be is a miracle in itself.

After many hours of writing and rewriting, sending emails and text messages, having Skype conversations, making phone calls, and receiving guidance from our Heavenly Father, *From Baptist Preacher to Mormon Teacher* is now a reality.

What you hold in your hands is a book that comes from the heart—both of our hearts—and has been written and shared with the intent to bring souls unto Christ, which, in the big picture, is what matters most.

Kelly L. Martinez
Coauthor

SECTION I

FROM

BAPTIST
PREACHER

CHAPTER 1

FROM STUDENT TO TEACHER

I F YOU'VE EVER watched *The Story Trek* on BYUtv, you know that everybody has a story. There's more to some than others, but that's mostly because of our ages, not the interest level of our lives. If given the chance to share their stories, most people shy away from the opportunity because they feel their life story isn't interesting enough. That's not true, though. Everybody's story is interesting because it's unique. No two stories are the same. They might be similar, but they are definitely not carbon copies.

There's a lot to my story, but I'll spare you all of the details and stick to what's most important to me—and hopefully to you.

My story—the part that matters most—began in 1977 when, at the age of eight, I had an out-of-body experience that changed my young life and set me on a path that, relatively speaking, not many black people have taken.

You'll see what I'm talking about later.

This life-altering experience happened while I was watching a preacher deliver a sermon at the Mt. Enon Missionary Baptist Church in Dayton, Ohio. It was as if the fast-forward button on my life was pressed, propelling me twenty years into the future where I saw myself preaching a sermon at a pulpit.

The vision was clear. It was real. It scared me.

I didn't understand why the vision was happening to a boy like me or what it meant. As far as I knew, only adults preached in church.

I wondered what, if given the chance, I would even say or how I would prepare to give a sermon. *How does any preacher go about it?* I wondered.

Nowadays, there are many children, even babies who can't form a complete sentence, preaching. Don't believe me? Do a quick search on YouTube.

But this was the 1970s; kids didn't preach in church. Ultimately, my fear of people not believing me, or making fun of me, won out, and I decided to keep the experience to myself. My game plan was to forget about it, which I *attempted* to do. However, things turned out to be different than I imagined. Several years later at the same church, a teenage boy in my Sunday School class told us that he was preparing to deliver a trial sermon.

In this particular Baptist church, when a person, even a child, felt called of God to preach the gospel, he or she informed the pastor of the experience right away. If, after consulting with the Lord, the pastor agreed with the person's calling, he scheduled a trial sermon.

You might think that if a fledgling preacher didn't perform well during a trial sermon, then that was the end of his preaching career. That wasn't necessarily true. If the sermon wasn't going well, the congregation chipped in, encouraging the preacher by shouting phrases like, "Take your time, baby!" or "Help 'em, Lord!" If that didn't help improve the sermon, then the pastor came to the rescue, and the trial sermon was over. This didn't invalidate the Lord's call for someone to preach; it just meant the novice preacher wouldn't deliver a sermon to that congregation anytime soon.

I'd seen this happen to several who thought they'd been called to preach, so the prospect of being in that situation frightened me.

If the trial sermon went well and the aspiring preacher reached the end of his sermon, then from that day forward he was addressed as reverend, and life was never the same. The respect that came with that title was intoxicating. It was as if the new preacher had become a rock star overnight.

This is precisely what happened to my Sunday School classmate. After nailing his trial sermon, the whole church was talking about him. He was a star.

This young man's success made it even more difficult for me to share my experience with the pastor. I was afraid that if I told him about it then, he'd think I was only trying to be like my classmate, wanting the attention and fame. Because I feared what people might think, I again chose to keep my calling to myself.

Not long after, I was sitting on my porch talking to a few of my neighborhood friends. Before I knew it, I was preaching to them. *Where did the words come from? How did I know what I was preaching? And what about the feeling of fire in my belly? Where did that come from?*

This happened regularly, and when it did, my friends bailed on me, saying, "Oh, no. There he goes again! Time to go home."

While I lacked the courage to act on the Lord's call to preach at church, I surely wasn't shy about preaching to my peers in a less formal setting.

WHEN I WAS growing up, it was common for kids in my neighborhood to grow up without a father in the home. In many cases, black men lacked the courage needed to be a good father and husband. Because my father was not part of my life, my childhood fit that mold. My father was a struggling musician. When I was conceived, he was married to another woman and had kids with her.

My mother lacked a stable man in her life, but she was a God-fearing woman. Sadly, she was plagued by paranoid schizophrenia and spent a large part of my childhood in a mental hospital, which proved to be very difficult for my younger brother and me.

Her mental illness didn't stop her from teaching me valuable things that continue to serve me today, though. One of the best things my mother taught me was to read the book of Proverbs in the Old Testament. The phrase "my son" is used often throughout that book and was familiar to me because it was the phrase my Father in Heaven used when He talked to me.

The more I read the scriptures, the more I began to develop a relationship with my Heavenly Father. I began to talk to Him regularly, and guess what? He talked to me too! Conversing with Him happened in a simple manner: I asked Him a question, and He answered, not audibly, but in my mind. His words simply flowed into my mind in response to my prayers. I know they were His words because they were accompanied by the power of the Holy Ghost.

I don't know why, but I chose to keep this relationship with Heavenly Father a secret. Looking back, it was good that I did because sometimes it's better to keep sacred things like that to yourself so others can't try to take them away from you or ridicule them.

All was not champagne wishes and caviar dreams in my home. I suffered from low self-esteem and lacked direction. Satan used my mother's mental illness against me, trying to convince me that I was just like her. Her illness frightened me, and Satan knew it.

On one occasion, my brother and I came home from school on a cold winter's day only to realize our mom had locked us out. She responded to my repeated knocking with a look from behind the drawn curtains that made it evident she didn't recognize us. She screamed at us to go away.

My brother and I tried to figure out what to do next. Eventually, we got cold enough to go to a neighbor's house for help. Our neighbor let us in, fed us, and listened to our story. I wound up calling our grandmother, who in turn called the police and paramedics. At the end of that sad situation, my mother was admitted to a mental hospital.

At the time, I understood my mother's mental illness to be a demonic spirit taking control of her. At least that's what the people at church said. Years later, I learned in a college psychology class that what my mother suffered from was called paranoid schizophrenia disorder. It humbled me to realize that for all those years I thought her behavior was something she had control over. For all those years, I was angry and hurt because I was told that the "demonic spirits" problem was something she'd brought on herself. I broke down and cried in that psychology class as it dawned on me that I could finally let go of the pain I'd carried over this for so many years.

This showed me that my mama was sick, not possessed by evil spirits. She had no way to know she was sick, either. You see, in my neighborhood, we didn't go to the doctor unless we were almost dead. Many of the families in my neighborhood were on welfare and most of the adults in those families didn't trust the doctors we had access to. So having my mother psychologically evaluated was out of the question.

As a child with the limited amount of knowledge I had about my mother's illness, I grew even more hesitant to share my calling from the Lord because I thought it would trigger something evil in her. The adults in my family referred to my mother's episodes as nervous breakdowns, which sugarcoated it for us kids but didn't really address the truth. In fact, they didn't really know the truth, but I think they knew it was something more than just a nervous breakdown.

A tender mercy for my family in the midst of my mother's struggles was that no matter what, we went to church. In spite of my mother's illness, she always found a way to put herself together enough to take us to church. I think this was a gift from my Father that helped keep me on the path to finding His true Church some day. Even with this tender mercy, it wasn't easy dealing with my mother's episodes.

The first breakdown I remember happened when I was about five or six years old. My mom put me in the bathtub, and my cousin must have thought I was in some kind of danger because he tried to come upstairs to get me. My mother filled a bucket with water and threw the water down the stairs at my cousin to keep him from coming up to get me. I don't remember—or maybe I didn't understand—what all was involved in that instance, but I do remember it scared me.

These types of episodes happened about once or twice a year. It got to the point where I could look into my mother's eyes and know she was about to have an episode. It scared me that the adult care-giver in my life would go so out of control. This created a deep desire in me to know God personally.

I contacted my mother shortly after that psychology class to share with her what I'd learned. We cried together, talked about it, and did quite a bit of healing after that. My mama still suffers from this disorder, but we deal with it much differently now. When God enlightens us with truth, we are able to heal—if we embrace that truth.

In spite of her mental illness, my mother was a very religious woman. I learned at a young age that in order to get along with her, I needed to talk about her favorite subject: God. I was okay with that because God and I were tight. Still are, in fact.

My mother was a church hopper, attending different churches over the years. If she didn't like what one preacher said, she'd visit another church until she found a preacher with whom she agreed. Her tendency to church hop helped me become familiar with different denominations.

In what proved to be a glimpse into my future, my mother and I once drove by an LDS meetinghouse in Trotwood, Ohio. I asked her why we never went to that church. Her answer surprised me and stayed with me for a long time. "Oh, baby," she said. "They don't allow black people in that church!"

Really? I made a mental note to avoid that church at all costs.

A particularly memorable conversation with my mother during my childhood came while we were getting ready for church one Sunday. I asked her how I would know if I was called by God to preach. "Well, son," she said, "ask God for something, and if He gives it to you, then take that as a sign that He's called you to preach."

"Okay, then I'll ask Him for a Jaguar."

She laughed and said I needed to be more specific.

"I'll ask Him for a red convertible Jaguar with chrome wheels!" She chuckled again, and I added, "Mom, if God wants me to preach, then all I need is for Him to provide me with His word. If He gives me a Bible, then I'll preach!"

We agreed it was a good idea, went to church, and didn't give it much thought after that.

As THEY HAVE a tendency to do, the years passed quickly. The next phase of my life worth sharing is my early adulthood when I joined the US Army. Uncle Sam stationed me in Germany during the late 1980s. As rich as Uncle Sam is, you'd think he could've sent me somewhere like Hawaii. But, like a good soldier, I went where I was told to go.

On a particular occasion, I was preparing to depart on a field maneuver and found myself in the PX (the Post Exchange store) gathering a few supplies to take with me. As I passed the magazine rack, I noticed a Bible sitting amongst the magazines. I thought it odd that a Bible would be there but decided to buy it so I could read it in the field.

In spite of my good intentions, I found the Bible at the bottom of my duffle bag when I returned from the field—unread. I placed it on my nightstand and paid it no attention for a few weeks. On an otherwise ordinary night, I sat on my bed, peering out my window into the dark of night, when my Heavenly Father spoke to me.

"You have the Bible you asked Me for," He said. "Now go and preach My word!" My Father was reminding me of the promise I'd made to Him with my mom several years earlier.

He spoke to me again: "You have the Bible you asked Me for. Now go preach My word!"

Memories of the promise I'd made with my mother sank into my soul at that moment, and I realized it was time for me to start my journey toward becoming a preacher. I'd neglected to follow through on that promise and calling, but I knew then that it was the time to get my act together.

I went to see the base chaplain the next morning and shared my spiritual experience with him. He said he didn't deal with mysticisms and referred me to Pastor Clemons, the Pentecostal pastor on base. Talk about passing the buck!

Pastor Clemons was more receptive when I shared my story, and he connected with me on many levels. So, I joined his church. Like the Baptist church back home, the Pentecostal church gave its preachers a trial sermon. I accepted the trial sermon assignment

FROM BAPTIST PREACHER TO MORMON TEACHER

Pastor Clemons gave me and delivered a discourse about how obedience is better than sacrifice, based on 1 Samuel 15:22. That sermon went well and was the first of many I delivered. It was official: I was a preacher. The hard part was over. Or so I thought.

***

As a preacher in the Pentecostal church, my title was minister. *Minister Myers!*

The Pentecostal ministry had several levels back then. Minister was the starting point, and then came elder. Some were called evangelists, and the titles went up to bishop. Some even referred to themselves as prophets or prophetesses.

Lineage played a role in a preacher's right to preach in the Pentecostal faith, but I never quite understood how that worked. It was good enough for me if the pastor gave me permission to preach and teach under his authority and direction.

In order to become an ordained minister, Pentecostal preachers had to meet with a board comprised of preachers and members of the congregation. This panel asked the candidate faith-based questions to determine if the person was qualified to preach. If the aspiring preacher passed the test, then ordination followed.

Interestingly, most Pentecostal preachers never got ordained, unless they wanted to become a pastor or a prison or hospital chaplain, or wanted to officiate at a wedding or funeral. This meant that many Pentecostal preachers were preaching to congregations across the country without having been ordained! This was the case when I was a Pentecostal preacher.

I preached in Germany for about a year before I started having questions about my role as one of God's servants. I felt that I should be doing and learning more.

An unexpected but profound teaching moment changed my course as a Pentecostal preacher—and as a disciple of Jesus Christ.

I, along with a few of my fellow ministers, regularly preached fire and brimstone to our fellow soldiers who we felt had not been saved. This was what we thought it meant to minister to our congregation.

While "ministering" to a few soldiers, one of them asked me a question.

"Myers, do you go to the hospital because you are well, or do you go because you are sick and need to *get* well?"

Arrogantly, I responded that one goes to the hospital because of illness in order to get well.

"Okay. Do you wash your hands when they are already clean, or do you wash them because they are dirty and need to be cleaned?" he followed up.

I was confused as to why this unsaved soldier was asking me questions to which the answers were obvious. "You wash your hands to get them clean, of course," I replied. "What's your point?"

In a humble manner, which was starkly contrary to my self-righteous attitude, the soldier told me that we are the same way when it comes to Jesus Christ. We seek Him to *become* clean, not because we *are* clean.

His words struck me deeply, and from that day on, I began to seek Christ more honestly and diligently so that I could come to the same understanding the soldier had already come to. It was as if the soldier's words flipped a switch inside of me and a light came on. I backed off preaching fire and brimstone after that. That conversation awakened a desire in me to know my Savior more intimately and to do His will more frequently.

I believe strongly that there are certain things that happen in our lives because our Heavenly Father guides us to them so He can put us on the right path. Whether it's a word, a phrase, a dream, or an experience, these things cause us to stop, ponder, and make needed changes. My conversation with the soldier was one of those experiences. It put me in the frame of mind where I started asking questions that caused the other ministers to doubt my commitment to the ministry, questions that led me farther down the path the Lord wanted me to travel.

CHAPTER 2

MY JOSEPH SMITH EXPERIENCE

ONE OF MY biggest concerns about being a minister was that I felt I wasn't growing or learning in my calling. Aside from delivering sermons, there wasn't much that fulfilled me as a preacher. I thought that there was more I should be doing. This mindset is not good for any situation, especially as a preacher.

During this trying time, Pastor Clemons invited me to his home for dinner. If there's one thing you can offer to make sure I'll come to visit, it's dinner. The invitation wasn't a surprise because it was well known that the pastor's daughter was a little sweet on me, and that the pastor's wife thought it was good for us to spend time together to get to know each another.

Shortly after arriving at the pastor's home, a thunderous knock on the door startled us as we were about to sit down to dinner. Where I come from, a knock that loud could only mean the police were at the door.

It turned out to be Pastor Mitchell from the Holiness church that was causing such a ruckus. He wasn't happy and demanded to know why Pastor Clemons was stealing members of his congregation. He was talking about me, but I was hardly a member of his congregation. I attended one service at his church shortly after arriving in Germany. Still, it wasn't a surprise to see these ministers contending with each other.

Perhaps a little background information would help you understand why seeing a Pentecostal and Holiness pastor argue over members was not that surprising. Pentecostal and Holiness church members strongly disagree about baptism, whether it should be done in the name of the Father, the Son, and the Holy Ghost, or in Christ's name only. This disagreement has led to many discussions that sadly turn into arguments.

Pastor Clemons decided to take the conversation into the hallway instead of allowing it to disrupt his family gathering. *Too late for that*, I thought. I offered to join him for support, but he said he could handle it himself. I felt responsible for the confrontation.

While the men continued yelling at each other in the hallway, Pastor Clemons's wife, bless her heart, tried to carry on as if nothing was wrong. Imagine this sweet woman trying to host a guest and put on a good face while her husband and a rival preacher—both supposedly men of God—were standing outside, yelling at each other. It was ironically humorous.

Eventually, Pastor Clemons returned and let us know all was well. *Really?* I thought. *Your raised voice and heated words could've fooled me!*

In spite of the pastor's reassurance, I felt terrible about being the cause of discord and realized I needed to do something to fix the situation. If my membership in these two churches was the cause of contention, then there must be a solution to the matter. If I was feeling torn between the two churches and pastors, I needed to find a way to decide which of them I should align myself with.

I decided to seek my Father's guidance about which church to attend.

I'D READ IN the Bible that God is not the author of confusion and that if I asked, it would be given me; if I sought, I would find; and if I knocked, He would open. Those promises meant something to me. They pointed me in the direction I should go when I needed to make an important decision. Like most of us, I didn't always think that way, but thankfully, I saw this as a situation that required me to exercise my faith in these promises.

So, I planned a camping excursion into the German wilderness to seek an answer about which church I should attend. A spiritual journey, you might call it. I skipped Friday-night prayer service, informing Pastor Clemons that I would not be in attendance because of my spiritual journey.

I headed for a castle in the German countryside, and when I got there, I started pitching my tent. I was *supposed* to be alone in the middle of nowhere that night. You can imagine my surprise when I heard low but clear voices talking behind me. This frightened me. There I was, a black man in the middle of the night in a German forest, and nobody knew where I was!

You fool, I thought. *Don't you know there are wild pigs in the German forest and that those low voices sound like Lucifer done sent his minions to make your spiritual journey a short one?*

On my hurried hike home from my ill-planned spiritual journey, I found the source of the low voices: fellow soldiers near the castle, drinking beer and enjoying the view. I visited with them for a few minutes and then hiked back to my room, where I could've spoken to my Father in the first place.

Some journey, I thought to myself. *I was gone all of two hours.*

<hr />

MY BEDSIDE WAS no Sacred Grove, but it was a place from which I knew my Father could hear me. I kneeled at my bedside that same night and asked my Father which of the two churches I should attend.

"Neither," He replied.

Not exactly the answer I was expecting, so I waited to hear more.

"Neither of those churches has the truth. They're both wrong."

Have you ever prayed about something and the answer you received from the Lord was so unexpected that you had to ask Him again? That's what it was like for me when I received this answer. One thing I'd learned by that point in my life was that if I was going to seek the Lord's counsel, I needed to trust in His words and do as He said. It was going to take a lot of faith this time, but I needed to press forward. I asked Him what He wanted me to do.

His answer came quickly and clearly: I was to inform Pastor Clemons that I would not be attending his church any longer and that I needed to wait until I returned to the United States for the Lord to lead me to His true Church.

I obeyed my Father and sought out Pastor Clemons the next day. When he saw me, he asked me to wait in the day room while he met with someone else. To my surprise, there was a group of my fellow preachers in the day room "ministering" to a young man, preaching fire and brimstone at him. They told him he was going to hell if he didn't change his life, stop listening to the devil's music, and start going to church.

That poor young man. The look on his face as he hung his head in shame made me well aware of the fact that I'd made people feel that way with my own aggressive preaching. While watching these preachers tear into this man, I realized that making someone feel poorly while trying to bully him into righteousness was not something Jesus would do, so why should a preacher, a supposed man of God? I decided right then that I would never do that to anyone again.

Pastor Clemons eventually entered the room and joined in the "saving" of this young man. He told the young man that he could be saved, but only if he would accept Jesus as his personal Savior and start going to church. The young man said he needed time to think about it, only to be torn into again by the ministers. Eventually, the young man left without being "saved" and the preachers discussed for a while how it was that they'd failed to convert the young man. If they'd asked my opinion, I would've told them why they had failed to convert the man, but I didn't think they would have received my opinion very well.

Then it was my turn.

"Minister Myers, what can I do for you?" asked Pastor Clemons.

I still liked the sound of that. *Minister Myers!* But rather than bask in my personal glory, I pressed forward. Based on what I'd witnessed moments before, I knew what I had to say wasn't going to go over well.

"Pastor Clemons," I started after taking a deep breath, "I've prayed about it and the Lord has told me not to attend your church any longer."

Pastor Clemons clasped his hands together as a hush fell over the room and asked, "Oh, really? And why is that?"

"After much prayer," I continued, "I was told that the truth is not in your church and that the Lord will guide me to His church when I return to the States."

There was a brief moment of silence, and then all H-E-double-hockey-sticks broke loose.

I was possessed by Satan. God told me no such thing. I was being deceived by the father of all lies. You get the idea. And then the other ministers chimed in with their two cents.

I stood my ground and did what my Father told me to do. I looked each of them in the eyes with the confidence that I knew—I *knew!*—that I was in the right because I was doing what God instructed me to do.

Pastor Clemons told me he couldn't wish God's blessings on me because of the mistake I was making. This hurt me to hear, but when I thought about it, it was what I expected. I bade farewell to and shook each of the ministers' hands and then left the building. I hung my head in sadness while I pondered what had just taken place. And then I felt the finger of the Lord lift my head up by the chin as He spoke to me. "My son, I am pleased with you. You did what I told you to do. Peace be unto you for following my instructions."

What could I say or think to contradict that? My Heavenly Father, the greatest of all, approved of what I had just done. There was nothing any man could say or do to me that could erase that moment. *Praise the Lord!* I thought as I continued to my room in the dark of night.

I only saw the ministers a few times after that, but for the most part, I had nothing to do with them. I had started down the path my Father pointed me to, and it was a lonely path to travel at first.

Soon after this experience, the military announced there was an overload in its ranks, which meant that those who wanted to get out of the army could do so. Eager to see where the Lord would lead me, I volunteered and took advantage of the announcement. In April 1990, I was on a plane headed back to the States.

CHAPTER 3

THE WRONG PATH

IF YOU'RE THINKING my path to the Lord's Church was smooth sailing after all that, you're mistaken.

When I got home from Germany, I was in sore need of a job. I had a wife, whom I married in 1989, and a child, who was born shortly after my wife and I got married. I was an honorably discharged veteran with a family, so things must've been peachy keen, right? Wrong.

Like many veterans, I found myself in the unemployment office, receiving coaching on how to get a job. My employment specialist was a nice young lady. She let me know that General Motors was hiring and that she thought I was a good candidate. Back then, a job with GM was a secure way to make a living. My, how times have changed!

Somewhere between looking at the job listing and evaluating my qualifications, the specialist changed gears and asked me what church I attended. *What's that got to do with getting me a job?* I thought. Doing my best to hide my surprise at the conversation's change of direction, I asked her how she knew I went to church.

"I can tell by your spirit," she replied.

I told her the name of the church I went to with my family while growing up but that I would not be attending that church anymore because I was waiting for the Lord to tell me what church I needed to attend.

FROM BAPTIST PREACHER TO MORMON TEACHER

All thoughts about GM and getting me a job left her mind at that point. Next thing I knew, she was going on and on about her church family and pastor. Her pastor was getting older and didn't have anyone to pass the congregation on to after he retired. He needed help, she said, and I should go with her to meet him.

I told her about how my calling to preach the Lord's word came to me as a child.

"I knew it! I just knew it!" she said with a Texas-sized smile. "God told me to help you!"

She continued expressing her belief that God had instructed her to help me and pledged to help me get that job at GM—which I did. She also knew I was going to like her pastor.

Maybe this is the church God promised to lead me to, I thought. I got my hopes up and decided to meet her pastor.

I realize now that I should've prayed about it first.

REVEREND J. A. Preston was a kindly man. I met him at his church the following Wednesday, right before noonday Bible study. The young lady was right; he was an elderly man and it was obvious he needed help at his church. I filled him in on the experiences I'd had on my path to the ministry and about the Lord's promise to lead me to His church upon my return to the States. I shared this with him because I wanted to be up front with him and certainly didn't want to repeat the fiasco I'd had in Germany with Pastor Clemons.

Reverend Preston decided to give me a try to see what happened. At the time, it seemed right, so I agreed to help him out.

I FEEL IT's right to bring up priestcraft at this point in my story. In its purest definition, *priestcraft* means the training, knowledge, and ability necessary to be a priest. It's the secondary definition of *priestcraft* I want to relate to the preaching experiences I had at this point in my life.

In the book of Alma in the Book of Mormon, a man named Nehor taught the people that preachers should be popular and supported by the people. This is the type of priestcraft that's popular today and that very much applied to the phase of my preaching I'm about to share. This type of priestcraft involves taking God's words and twisting them to manipulate others into giving you money to support your personal financial gain. I put this form of priestcraft in the same category as witchcraft. Priestcraft is a wicked and ancient practice that's also a method the devil uses to lead the children of God astray. This is the very thing I found myself involved in at this point in my life.

I BECAME A member of Reverend Preston's church right away, and we scheduled my initial sermon for soon thereafter. The reverend didn't like the term *trial sermon* because he didn't think it was right that the members put a man preaching the word of God on trial.

My initial sermon went well, and the members were receptive. And then it happened, slowly, gently, and almost unnoticeably. I started getting paid to preach, which was a game-changer for me. I felt bad about getting paid to preach. It felt wrong. Money took the purity away from what I was doing, but I took it anyway.

It felt like dirty money, but I needed the cash, so I found a way to justify my actions. It never got easier to take the money, and I was never comfortable with it, but the dollars found their way into my bank account.

Along with the money came preaching opportunities at other churches and a lifestyle that was contrary to the principles by which a preacher should conduct himself. Before I knew it, I was so deeply involved in unrighteous living that I no longer felt worthy to preach, but I continued anyway. This made everything about being a preacher worse than I could imagine. I was a hypocrite, and I knew it. I was off course, and it wasn't pretty.

I started carrying a .357 snub-nosed pistol for protection because I was going places I shouldn't have been going, and I felt unsafe. I don't know how much of a real threat there was, but in my mind, I needed to carry a weapon.

I also began entertaining thoughts of suicide. Things had gotten so bad that I found myself driving around one night in search of a spot to end my hypocrisy with one pull of the .357's trigger. I didn't want this kind of lifestyle. How did things get so bad so quickly? I was supposed to be a man of God!

It had been five years since I met the woman in the unemployment office, and things had gotten really bad. I needed to make some changes, but I didn't know how to make them.

To make matters worse, my marriage was falling apart and we did nothing to save it. My wife and I eventually separated, and the child support was a huge financial burden. If it weren't for the money I received for preaching, I don't know how I would have survived. I felt trapped in the life I'd built for myself and knew that I was cheating God. There seemed to be no way out of the hole I'd dug for myself.

Things at church started getting bad too. Reverend Preston benched me, to borrow a sports term, and didn't tell me about it. Like a star athlete, being benched as a preacher meant I didn't get into the preaching game anymore. My lifestyle made it so I didn't even realize I was benched at Reverend Preston's church until the lady I met at the unemployment office asked me when I was going to preach at her church again. My life was a mess.

In an attempt to get some direction in my life, I sought the help of a fellow preacher, the same one I mentioned earlier from my youth, the one who became a rock star in the preaching world as a teenager. I thought he'd have some answers for sure! Sadly, his answers weren't the ones I was looking for or needed. He suggested I go out of town with him to indulge in my sinful ways so that nobody knew who I was and so that the members of the church wouldn't see me. Talk about the blind leading the blind!

I sought advice from other preachers too and learned that each dealt with the same problem but in different ways. None of their ways satisfied me, and I soon decided to leave the ministry forever. I don't mean to imply that every preacher leads a sinful lifestyle, but many of the ones I associated with did.

I was at my wit's end. I had to find a way to stop abusing my relationship with my Heavenly Father. I loved Him and wanted nothing more than to please Him. I knew—I *knew*—that He wasn't pleased with my behavior. My heart ached for what I was doing.

I decided to preach one last sermon the following Sunday, and then my preaching career would be over. I'd be a retired preacher.

I'd taken a job as a bus driver for the Miami Valley Regional Transit Authority by this time, so I started taking Sunday shifts to justify my absence at church. A few months passed and eventually the invitations to preach stopped and people quit looking for me at church.

Thankfully, that nightmare of a detour on my path to the Lord's true Church came to an end, but not without its casualties, including my marriage.

CHAPTER 4

THE LOVE BUS

Monday, June 26, 1995, at 10:05 p.m. was a date and time that changed my life. It wasn't an out-of-body experience, but it was a moment in which I felt my Father in Heaven direct me.

I was still driving a bus for the Miami Valley Regional Transit Authority. I was on a layover break before turning my bus around to drive the same route I had just completed, but in the opposite direction.

I liked to read books on my breaks and was doing so when, out of the corner of my eye, I noticed a young lady with two kids boarding the bus. As she passed by me, I got a feeling I never had before but was somehow familiar.

The feeling was similar to the story in Mark 5 when the woman touched the hem of Jesus's garment and He immediately felt virtue go out of His body. Except with my experience, I felt virtue go *into* my body as she walked by. The feeling was so strong that it caused me to look up to see who had made me feel that way.

When I looked up and saw her, I recognized her as the girl I dreamed about as an adolescent. An adolescent boy dreaming about girls is nothing new, but the dream I had was different than just an average teenager's fantasy. I didn't see her face in my dream, only the back of her. The dream was so powerful that when I woke up, I knew I needed to make finding that girl a priority.

I pushed the memory of my boyhood dream aside for a moment and started prepping the bus for departure. As I did so, I couldn't help but think that after years of *looking* for the girl of my dreams, maybe I should have been *feeling* for her instead. It blew my mind to think I finally found my dream girl. I couldn't take my eyes off of her.

As He had many times during my life, my Heavenly Father spoke to my mind, right there while I was turning the bus around.

"That's your wife," He said.

How could this be? I thought. *I'm still married and in the middle of a divorce!*

"The wife you have now is the one *you* chose," the Lord said to me. "This is the wife *I* chose for you!"

Of the many conversations I had with my Father over the years, this one was the strangest. I mean, why would God talk to me in this manner while I was still married to another woman? I didn't know why, but I figured that God's ways are not man's ways, so I rolled with it. I heard God's voice enough in my life to know when He was speaking to me.

As I processed what He had spoken to me, I glanced over at the young lady and thought she looked like she'd put in a full day's work and was in no mood for flirting.

Father, I thought, *you're gonna have to tell her she's the one for me, because she don't look like she wanna hear it from me!*

"Tell her she has a beautiful spirit," He replied.

What? That's the best you got, Father? You're trying to be my wing-man and the best you can give me is to tell her she has a beautiful spirit?

"Just tell her."

So I leaned closer to the young lady and said, "Excuse me, miss. You have a beautiful spirit." She blushed, and her smile lit up the bus, and my heart.

Yes, Lord! You always know what to say! I gushed heavenward in my mind.

We exchanged names—hers was Sebrina—and talked as we rode through downtown. As fate would have it, her stop was the one where my shift ended and another driver took over the route.

I walked her and her kids to their transfer stop. It became a routine that repeated itself every Monday night over the next few months.

That night, on a public transportation bus, was the best night of my life to that point. I even wrote a song about Sebrina and that night. I'm happy to sing it for whoever will listen.

Then again, maybe we can just shake hands and call it good.

WEEKS LATER ON our weekly bus trip, I noticed Sebrina was reading something, so I asked her what it was.

"A Relief Society manual."

"Relief Society?" I asked. "What's that?" I thought maybe she was a member of The Order of the Eastern Star, or some organization like that.

"It's from my church," she replied.

My attempt to look intelligent by asking what she was reading faded quickly. I tried to recover by asking what church she attended.

"I'm a member of The Church of Jesus Christ of Latter-day Saints," she replied.

I'd never heard of that church before, but its name sounded familiar, like one I'd seen on a late-night commercial about families or something like that.

"Some people call us Mormons," she continued.

Oh, I'd heard that name before! "No way!" I chimed back. "There's no such thing as black Mormons!" The memory of my mother and I driving by the Mormon church house in my youth came to mind.

"Well, now you've met one."

I couldn't believe I met one of those people who drive horse-drawn buggies down the street. Her smile faded as she shook her head. "Those are the Amish." The only way to save face at this point was to ask Sebrina to tell me about her church and some of its teachings. She said she'd only been a member a short while and didn't want to give me any wrong information. But if I really wanted to learn more, she'd be happy to cook me dinner and have a couple of her better-qualified friends join us to tell me about the Church.

How could I refuse an offer like that? Before I accepted, however, curiosity reared its head. "How can you belong to a church you can't explain?"

She said she was still learning and was afraid she might say something that wasn't right. I still didn't understand, but I knew it was best not to press the matter. So dinner it was, friends and all.

CHAPTER 5

SEBRINA'S STORY

O N A MONDAY night in 1993, Sebrina dropped to her knees to offer a prayer that she knew her Heavenly Father would answer some day. What she didn't know was that He would answer it the next day. His answer marked the beginning of a journey that led to many spiritual and temporal miracles.

Her prayer was not a general prayer that gets offered absent-mindedly or when trouble comes knocking. This prayer was a specific, heartfelt prayer in which she asked God to send someone to share the scriptures with her. Her life was not easy at the time, and she wanted help from heaven in the form of God's word. She made plenty of mistakes in her life to that point, for which she asked God to forgive her. She also wanted to know what God's will was for her life and wanted Him to show her how to go down that path. She wanted another chance to put her life in accordance with God's will and felt the scriptures held the answer—but she needed help.

The following morning, at 10:57 a.m., a knock on her door startled Sebrina. She looked through the peephole and saw two young men in suits with black name tags that said Jesus Christ in big white letters. Her heart pounded within her as she realized that this—this very moment—was the answer to the prayer she offered the night before.

She paused with her back against the door for what seemed to her to be a long time. She was nervous about what the answer to her prayer might entail. She wondered if she'd be able to live up to the challenge.

The young man knocked again, this time a little louder. Sebrina looked down at her clothes and thought she wasn't dressed appropriately to greet men of God at the door, but she cracked the door open slightly anyway.

"Hello?" she asked apprehensively.

The young men identified themselves and asked if she had ever heard of the Book of Mormon. Her heart leaped for joy within her, but she worked hard to conceal it. The young men offered to teach her about the book and how it related to Jesus Christ. Sebrina told them it would be better for them to come back another time.

This is best, she thought. *I have things to do right now and want to be sure to give Jesus all of my attention.* They gave her a copy of the book and made an appointment to come back when it was more convenient.

At their first appointment, it didn't take long for her to realize that these representatives of Jesus Christ had a divine message for her. The young men taught her about Joseph Smith's First Vision, and after they left, she prayed to God to know if, indeed, Joseph was a prophet. The Spirit spoke to her clearly, testifying that what the young men taught her was true. She recognized the feeling of warmth and love she felt during that prayer. It was the same feeling she'd felt when she was fourteen and prayed for comfort and the ability to focus on her new task in life, which at the time was the start of her high school years.

In later meetings, the young men—ironically called elders—taught her more about the Book of Mormon and the church with which it was associated—The Church of Jesus Christ of Latter-day Saints. As the lessons progressed, Sebrina became familiar with the plan of salvation, a kind and loving plan that Heavenly Father implemented with the help of His Son, Jesus Christ. The elders also taught her about the war in heaven, a story she'd heard as a little girl but was unable to find in the Old Testament. Because she couldn't find the story in the scriptures, she had, over the years, started to doubt the account even existed.

Her heart filled with joy as she felt the doubts melt away each time the missionaries came to visit.

During the fourth lesson, Sebrina listened to her teachers as they explained in greater detail about how the Book of Mormon had come to pass. During the lesson, they read a passage that the elders weren't sure she understood.

> And he had caused the cursing to come upon them, yea, even a sore cursing, because of their iniquity. For behold, they had hardened their hearts against him, that they had become like unto a flint; wherefore, as they were white, and exceedingly fair and delightsome, that they might not be enticing unto my people the Lord God did cause a skin of blackness to come upon them. (2 Nephi 5:21)

When asked if she understood the scripture, Sebrina confidently said she did. She noticed the elders' countenances change and sadness come over them. They explained that there was a time in the Church's history when blacks could not hold the priesthood.

In the face of this news, her thoughts turned immediately to Proverbs 3:5: "Trust in the Lord with all thine heart; and lean not unto thine own understanding."

What the missionaries had taught her up to this point had pricked her heart, and she believed strongly in their words. She didn't understand why the priesthood had been withheld from black men, but she was willing to put all of her trust in the feelings of the Spirit that had touched her so strongly. She suggested they stay away from the topic for the time being until God would help her understand.

The elders agreed and proceeded to teach her about other truths found in the Book of Mormon. She learned a lot about faith from the prophet Alma in the book of Alma, and continues to do so to this day.

She didn't agree with all of the elders' interpretations of the scriptures, but she saw the fruits of their labors and trusted that they were called of God. She continued praying about the things she learned from the missionaries, and each time she prayed, she received a witness that this was the Lord's Church.

FROM BAPTIST PREACHER TO MORMON TEACHER

Eventually, she accepted the missionaries' invitation to be baptized and became a member of The Church of Jesus Christ of Latter-day Saints.

CHAPTER 6

THE WHITE GUYS WITH THE NAME TAGS

L ET'S GET ON with the story, then. Don't worry, Sebrina will make plenty of appearances along the way. So, where were we? Ah, yes: my dinner date with the most beautiful girl in the world—and her friends.

I arrived at Sebrina's home bright-eyed and bushy-tailed. Why shouldn't I have been? I was on cloud nine, thinking of the possibilities that lay ahead for us as a couple.

One of the first things I noticed in the apartment—besides my dream girl—was what looked like a book of scripture. It was too small to be the Bible, but there was no mistaking that is was a religious book. The book—the Book of Mormon—was sitting on the center table, so I asked her if I could take a look at it. She said I couldn't because I had to wait for her friends to arrive.

I didn't like the sound of that. First she wouldn't tell me anything about her church, and then I couldn't look at a book that was obviously on the table for people to look at. Maybe I'd entered the Twilight Zone. Besides, my peeking at the book wouldn't spoil anything, but she insisted that I wait.

Finally, two young white guys wearing white shirts, ties, and black name tags on their shirt pockets showed up. *These teenagers can't possibly be our teachers for the evening*, I thought.

The first missionary offered his hand, followed by the other. I shook their hands skeptically. You see, I was still an arrogant, know-it-all preacher. These juveniles surely didn't have anything spiritual to offer me.

Cordial small talk soon gave way to Sebrina's delicious dinner. The first missionary, who quickly became *my* missionary, and I hit it off pretty well from the start. I noticed a calm spirit about the young men and appreciated that. We talked basketball, which was something we had in common and was a good icebreaker. I shared the story about how Sebrina and I had met, which led to questions about the Church and about why Sebrina wanted them to teach me instead of teaching me herself.

Those poor missionaries. As I look back across the canyon of time, I'm sure they sensed my disdain and doubt. I'm so glad they were brave enough to continue with their message.

My missionary asked if I'd ever heard of Joseph Smith, and I said I hadn't. He started to teach me about Joseph. Stillness came upon the room, and I felt the Holy Spirit in a fullness that I'd never felt before. Tears ran down my face as he told me about the boy Joseph's confusion over which church to join and how, after reading James 1:5, he decided to retreat into the woods—sound familiar?—to ask God which church he should join.

Then my missionary read Joseph's words: "Never did any passage of scripture come with more power to the heart of man than this did at this time to mine" (Joseph Smith—History 1:12). I was mesmerized as my missionary related how Joseph's retreat into the woods in search of the truth differed from mine:

> After I had retired to the place where I had previously designed to go, having looked around me, and finding myself alone, I kneeled down and began to offer up the desires of my heart to God. I had scarcely done so, when immediately I was seized upon by some power which entirely overcame me, and had such an astonishing influence over me as to bind my tongue so that I could not speak. Thick darkness gathered around me, and it seemed to me for a time as if I were doomed to sudden destruction.
>
> But, exerting all my powers to call upon God to deliver me out of the power of this enemy which had seized upon me, and at the very moment when I was ready to sink into despair and abandon myself to destruction—not to an imaginary ruin, but to the power of some actual being from the unseen world, who had such marvelous

power as I had never before felt in any being—just at this moment of great alarm, I saw a pillar of light exactly over my head, above the brightness of the sun, which descended gradually until it fell upon me.

It no sooner appeared than I found myself delivered from the enemy which held me bound. When the light rested upon me I saw two Personages, whose brightness and glory defy all description, standing above me in the air. One of them spake unto me, calling me by name and said, pointing to the other—This is My Beloved Son. Hear Him! (Joseph Smith—History 1:15–17)

I was enthralled as my missionary continued, revealing that Joseph was instructed to not join any of the churches. There's more to Joseph's story, but I won't go into the details here. I encourage all who haven't read it—and even those who have—to read the rest of the story. The Spirit is strong in Joseph's words, and you can come to know of their truthfulness by praying to God for a witness. One of the many beauties of the truth is that God will manifest it to you again and again, whether it's your first time asking or your millionth time asking.

By the end of the story, there wasn't a dry eye in the room. My missionary asked me how I felt when he shared Joseph's story. I told him I felt the Spirit strongly and knew that what he taught me was true because I'd had a similar experience in my search for the truth, which I shared with them. I told them that I knew this was the church my Father told me He would lead me to. This tidbit of information surprised all three of my dinner companions, especially Sebrina. I guess I hadn't told her everything about my experiences at that point.

I was what missionaries call "golden." I accepted the truth openly and wholeheartedly. I was the type of person full-time missionaries dream about finding on their missions.

I wanted to know what I had to do to become a member of the LDS Church and when I could be baptized. My missionary tried to slow my roll a bit by telling me I had to gain a testimony of the Book of Mormon first, not to mention take the other five discussions. He handed me a copy of the Book of Mormon—more willingly than Sebrina did with her copy—and I started reading right away. As I read and pondered what I was reading, Father spoke to me confirming that what I was reading was scripture.

"What else do I need to do?" I asked my tutors.

<hr/>

THIS IS THE part where the enemy steps in to try and spoil the good that had been done in my heart. He tried to discourage me even before I accepted baptism into the Lord's true Church.

I made an appointment to meet with the elders a few days after our first meeting. After the elders left that night, Sebrina said there was something she needed to tell me. You men out there know that anytime a woman says she has something to tell you, what comes next usually ain't good.

"I want to be the one to tell you this," she said, "because I don't want you to feel duped after you join the church."

Uh-oh, I thought.

"There was a time in the history of the LDS Church when black men could not hold the priesthood."

Screech! Hold up! First off, what is this priesthood? And why couldn't black men hold it?

"The priesthood is the power and authority from God to act in His name. It's given to worthy male members of the Church. As for why black men couldn't hold the priesthood, I don't know."

A moment of silence, please. This is a difficult memory to recount . . .

Okay. Deep breath. Let's continue.

I felt like someone had thrust a fist into my chest and ripped out my heart. It took all I had to keep from breaking down in tears right then and there. How could God have led me to His true Church only to find out it was a racist church? How could anyone—a church much less—justify withholding such power from a man because of the color of his skin? How could this type of church really be true if the scriptures clearly say that God is no respecter of persons?

It didn't make sense to me. I was devastated. I couldn't wait to give those elders a piece of my mind.

THE WHITE GUYS WITH THE NAME TAGS

THE SITUATION TOOK me back to the disappointments I experienced in my childhood.

I mentioned earlier that I grew up without a father in my life. Every once in a while he visited, but for the vast majority of time, I waited for visits that never came.

My mother had an ugly, uncomfortable pink chair with oversized arms on it that sat in the living room next to the front window. On Friday nights, I started a vigil in that chair, looking out the window with hope that my father would show up as he promised he would. With each approaching car, my heart fluttered with excitement, hoping he was coming to pick me up, only to have my hopes dashed each and every time.

I often fell asleep in the chair, waiting for my father, only to awaken in the morning to continue the watch-and-wait routine. After watching hundreds of cars pass by over the weeks, months, and years, I grew tired of my heart breaking with every passing car and eventually stopped hoping.

Years later, I learned that my mother cried on her bed every time I started my weekend ritual waiting for my father. It not only broke my heart, but it broke hers too. As we all know, a mother's broken heart hurts doubly. It hurts for herself, but it hurts even more for her child. This might be the reason she introduced me to my Father in Heaven through the Bible when I was a preteen. I especially loved reading Proverbs and fell in love with every word. In them, my hope was born again. Through those words, I came to know my Heavenly Father, the greatest father I have ever known. In those words, I found trust and gained a testimony that my Father in Heaven would always show up and would always keep His word. With His word came power to overcome any and every obstacle the devil put in my way. Up to that point in my life, my Father had *never* let me down.

Until now, I thought.

I had a host of questions about the information Sebrina dropped on me.

How could the God of Abraham, Isaac, and Jacob—the Father I had come to know so well over the years—turn out to be a respecter of persons? How could He—who had protected me, cared for me, and been there for me when nobody else was—keep His authority and power from some of His children because of the color of their skin, which He created and gave to them?

I was born into that skin—am still wrapped in it, actually. I found it hurtful that my Father, the Omnipotent One, was at one point a racist and had only changed His way of thinking about people of color like me in the not-too-distant past. (More on this later. Stay tuned.)

I asked Sebrina how she could be a part of a racist church like this one.

"I know the Church is true and that some of the members do not understand that man's ways are not God's ways," she said. "I believe those racist teachings came from man and not God!"

I agreed with her perspective, but I was still heated, to say the least. I wanted answers. *Just wait until I see those missionaries,* I thought.

A FEW DAYS later, I returned to Sebrina's house to meet with the missionaries for our second discussion. I was a confused and hurt investigator—and I was ready to explode.

Before I let you in on the details of our meeting, let me make it clear how sensitive this topic is for investigators of color—and many others, actually. I don't think many Church members and missionaries realize how much this topic hurts us. I knew in my heart that something was wrong with this past practice regarding black men and the priesthood. As a black man, I had been judged and treated poorly throughout my life for no other reason than the color of my skin. I knew the word of God, I knew Him, and I knew that this practice wasn't right.

Like many investigators of the LDS Church, I had a limited understanding of Christ's love, and that love is the key ingredient in all of the teachings of His gospel. As a black man and investigator with limited knowledge of Christ's love, I was ready for war.

I showed up for our appointment a little early and waited impatiently for the elders to arrive. Finally, a knock on the door announced their arrival, and Sebrina showed them into the living room. It irritated me that they were so happy and perky, but I forced a friendly greeting and handshake before tearing into them.

"So, Elder," I said accusingly before our rear sides even hit our seats, "why is it that black men couldn't hold the priesthood?" My forced smile morphed into an icy stare while I waited for him to reply.

My missionary's face went pale, then blotchy red as he gave Sebrina a confused look as if to say, "What did you do? He was ready to be baptized when we left! Now this?"

Sebrina turned her head as if to respond, "Hey, I got him here. It's your job to answer his questions."

My elder composed himself and responded with a scripture. We turned to 2 Nephi 5:21 (yes, this is the same scripture Sebrina dealt with while being taught by the missionaries):

> And he had caused the cursing to come upon them, yea, even a sore cursing, because of their iniquity. For behold, they had hardened their hearts against him, that they had become like unto a flint; wherefore, as they were white, and exceedingly fair and delightsome, that they might not be enticing unto my people the Lord God did cause a skin of blackness to come upon them.

This didn't help the situation; it only angered me more. "So, you're telling me that black people are cursed?" I spat back.

Without missing a step, my missionary gave an emphatic, "Yes!"

All H-E-double-hockey-sticks broke loose then. I couldn't believe what I was hearing. *This white boy done lost his mind!* I thought as I showed the elders the door. "Okay, meeting over. I've heard enough!" Yes, I kicked those elders out of Sebrina's house. I was so upset that I had to excuse myself and went home for the night.

At home, I fell to my knees and cried to my Heavenly Father for what seemed like hours. *Why?* I asked Him. *Why would you lead me to the church you promised to lead me to only for me to find out they practiced racism in the past?* I was angry, hurt, frustrated, and sad all at the same time. I thought that my faith had been shattered.

One thing kept replaying in my mind, though: Joseph Smith's encounter with God and His Son, Jesus Christ. I knew it was true. I had felt it, and my Father had confirmed it to me. I am so grateful for my own Joseph Smith experience, because I don't think I could have overcome this hurdle without it.

What bothered me even more was that the Church seemed to be teaching racism from the heart of the book it said was another testament of Jesus Christ: The Book of Mormon. The Jesus I knew was no respecter of persons and died for all of us, not just the white folks. How could this be? I prayed and cried well into the night, pleading for my Father to help me understand this contradiction.

His words came to me as they had many times before. "My son, all your life you've been taught and told that you can't do things because of your skin color. Others have held you back because you believe what they say about you. I have fulfilled the promise I made to you in Germany by leading you to My true Church, and you have received a witness from Me that it's true. If you're going to let your skin color and the way others view your skin color stop you from accepting the truth, then all we've done together will have been for nothing. If you trust Me and continue with the lessons on to baptism, I'll teach you what My true doctrine means."

God's words were good enough for me. I'm not saying I totally embraced what I perceived to be racism, but I trusted that the Lord would keep His word and eventually teach me to understand.

I called Sebrina the next morning to tell her what happened, and then I contacted the elders to reschedule our appointment. At our next meeting, I told them about my conversation with the Lord and told them that we should stay away from the topic of blacks and the priesthood. I let them know that Father promised me He would explain things to me as I progressed in my understanding of the gospel and gained a testimony.

Without hesitation and with a huge amount of relief, the elders agreed to my terms.

Softening your heart after you've had your pride stomped on or been insulted by someone is not easy to do. However, because my Father helped me, my heart was receptive to the truths my missionary friends taught me.

MY LESSONS CONTINUED and I got to know the members of Sebrina's ward, the local congregation. I was impressed with what I saw. They were good people and practiced what they preached.

One member—"Doc," as Sebrina affectionately called him—wanted to get to know me a little better so he could see what my intentions were with Sebrina. He invited us to his house for dinner. Doc and his family lived in Centerville, Ohio, a part of town that most black people avoided because of reported police harassment. Few blacks lived in Centerville, and the ones that did were considered "sell-outs" by most black people. I'd never received a dinner invitation to a Caucasian's home before then.

I was a bundle of nerves when we rang the doorbell. Doc's wife answered the door, greeted us warmly, and then did something I was not prepared for—she turned and walked away! I was like a deer caught in headlights. I didn't know what to do. Here was a Caucasian woman I'd never met before, inviting me—a black man—into her home and leaving me basically on my own without keeping an eye on me to make sure I didn't steal anything!

Sebrina looked at me with that look that only a black woman can give with her teeth clamped together while moving her lips. "Come on, and stop acting like you ain't never been nowhere before!"

"I ain't moving until she comes back," I whispered in reply. "Ain't nobody gonna say I stole nothing!"

Sebrina shook her head, clamped her teeth even more, and motioned for me to follow her, which I did like I was one of her kids.

Doc introduced himself to me and shook my hand while his wife put the finishing touches on dinner. We made small talk, and then he cut to the chase. "So, Wain, what are your plans with Sebrina?" I was shocked but shouldn't have been. Sebrina warned me that Doc was protective of her.

"We're taking it slow," I told him, because we'd both been previously married and neither marriage worked out. Doc said he was familiar with Sebrina's ex and that her last encounter with him landed her in the hospital, where Doc personally put armed security on her room. He emphasized the *armed* part. Our conversation made it clear that these folks really cared about each other and were willing to look out for one another. Their love for each other was grounded in the gospel of Jesus Christ.

WHEN I INVESTIGATED the Church in the mid-1990s, the missionaries taught six discussions, or lessons. I had to receive each of the discussions before I could get baptized. During these discussions, the elders invited me to attend church services. They explained to me that LDS church services were held on Sundays in a three-hour block of meetings.

First came sacrament meeting, where members partook of the sacrament to renew their baptismal covenants. Members of the congregation then delivered sermons from the pulpit during this meeting as well. My tutors informed me that there was no paid clergy in the Church and that the same person did not preach to the congregation each week. This was huge to me, given my feelings and experience in regard to being paid to preach. I was fine with that, but the music? Well, I was a little shocked by that.

How can I put this gently? The music stunk, to say the least. No drums, no choir, no soloist, and, to me, no spirit. Where were the spiritual movement, clapping, and Church members shouting "Amen"? Was the music in the LDS Church intended for a funeral?

I kept all of these thoughts to myself. I was an investigator, after all. So I stuck to investigating.

And then there were the talks. Oh. My. Goodness. Can you say *boring*? *These Mormons need some help*, I thought. I had no idea who they were talking about. They couldn't possibly have been talking about Jesus Christ, Mary's baby, Immanuel, King of kings, or the Lord of lords. *Can I get an "amen" up in here?*

I had to stop and remind myself I was an investigator. *No rocking the boat your first week, Wain.* Hey, you can take the Baptist out of the preacher, but you can't take the preacher out of the man!

Next came Sunday School, where I attended the investigators class, also known as the Gospel Essentials class. This was my favorite of the three meetings, and still is to this day. It was simple and easy to understand. I'm surprised more members don't attend this class. It's a great way to review the basics. Besides, the Spirit can teach us something new no matter which class we attend, right?

The teacher asked me to give the opening prayer, and I can still remember the experience like it was yesterday. I opened my prayer in classic Baptist-preacher fashion, with all the trimmings. As I prayed, it seemed to me that my classmates weren't feeling it. No "Amen!" No "Thank you, Jesus!" No cheering section. *What's wrong with these people?* For being members of Father's true Church, they needed some work in the praise and worship department.

At the end of class, a brother—not a *brutha*—stood to offer the closing prayer, and he flat out talked to God like they were buddies. When he concluded his prayer, everyone said "Amen" and thanked him for such a good prayer. *What in the world is going on? I'm going to have to help these people find the Holy Ghost and feel the Spirit, because they are missing the mark.*

The third and final meeting in the block was priesthood meeting. This meeting is where all of the priesthood holders in the congregation gather to make announcements and report on activities. This group is comprised of all male members age twelve and up. This announcement and reporting portion of the meeting is known as opening exercises. *Funny,* I thought, *no jumping jacks, no toe touches, but they call it exercises?*

After opening exercises, the priesthood holders separated into smaller groups, called quorums, based mostly on age. I was told to go meet with the elders quorum, where the quorum leaders followed up on assignments and a teacher gave a lesson. Before I knew it, it was time to go.

Wow! A brutha could get used to this! I was used to being in church all day on Sunday, so all my issues with the music, talks, and lack of a cheering section went right out the door. These meetings only went three hours! They started on time and ended on time. These white folks were onto something after all.

After church services, the missionaries took me to meet the congregation's leader, Bishop Weston. In the LDS Church, a bishop is a lay ecclesiastical leader who is chosen from among the male members of the congregation. Church members have a lot of respect for their bishop.

Bishop Weston said he'd like to meet with me but was booked with appointments that day, so we made an appointment for later that week. I was excited to get to meet a leader in the Lord's true Church.

Our meeting time arrived, and he invited me into his office, which was very plain and simple: a few chairs, a desk, fluorescent lighting, and a few pictures on the walls. Nothing flashy, just what was necessary for people to visit. Bishop Weston got straight to the point and told me how much Sebrina meant to him and his family and that they wanted the best for her. He also expressed his love for the Savior and His church.

I noticed something strange happening while he spoke: Bishop Weston had tears running down his face. No sobbing, no runny nose, no trying to regain composure. Just tears running down his face as he talked in what appeared to be his normal tone of voice. Now, I'd seen crying without tears, but I'd never seen tears without crying. I asked him why he had tears running down his face. I thought he might have some kind of condition or something.

Bishop Weston smiled and said that whenever he spoke of the Savior, he couldn't stop the tears from falling. This amazed me, and I thought it was one of the most genuine outpourings of the Spirit that I'd ever witnessed. I hoped that one day I'd be able to share in those uncontrolled tears that came without crying.

While I investigated the Church, I found a few things lacking, but most of all, I felt the Spirit in all things pertaining to the Church and saw its fruits—which were precious and beautiful! After meeting with the bishop and the missionaries and attending services, I knew that my days of investigating the Lord's true Church had come to an end.

AFTER FINISHING ALL six of the missionary discussions, I was interviewed for baptism by a missionary I'd never met before. He wanted to make sure I understood what I was getting into and that I had a basic knowledge of the gospel—a quality control measure, you might call it. That elder cleared me for baptism, and we made plans for my baptismal service. I was excited to finally receive this sacred ordinance from someone who had the proper authority.

By this time, Sebrina and I had become regulars at Doc's house. We were having dinner with Doc, his wife, and the missionaries when my missionary let us know that he'd made a goal to baptize someone in Doc's swimming pool before the end of his mission. Doc told him that if he found someone ready for baptism to let him know and he'd make it happen.

The Spirit whispered to me to volunteer to be the one baptized in Doc's pool, so I did. My missionary thought I was kidding, but I was serious. And so it was. On August 25, 1995, I was baptized by the same authority that the Savior Himself bestowed upon His Apostles. Memories of this life-changing day still bring tears to my eyes twenty years later.

MANY CHURCH MEMBERS came to my baptismal service, packing the streets around Doc's house with their cars. Each had come to show their love and support for a Baptist preacher who accepted the teachings of the Lord's true Church: The Church of Jesus Christ of Latter-day Saints.

The service only lasted about forty-five minutes, but they were a powerful forty-five minutes. After an opening prayer and song, my missionary led me down into the waters of baptism—Doc's swimming pool.

One of the service's highlights for me was the talk my missionary gave before baptizing me. He read a letter that told a story about two friends who, in the premortal life, learned their time to go to earth had arrived. One of these friends was to be born into prosperity and a family that had the gospel and priesthood, while the other would be born into poverty and without the gospel. With tears in his eyes, the friend who'd been assigned to a family without the gospel pleaded with his friend to find him on earth and to bring him the gospel. The fortunate friend promised he would. Eventually the pair met on earth, and both rejoiced as they realized that the fortunate one had indeed kept his promise—he'd found his friend!

My missionary and I cried like babies at this point. We both felt the Spirit and knew we had been friends in premortality and that he was like the friend who'd been born into the gospel and prosperity while I was the one who was born into poverty and an absence of the gospel. I was his friend and he'd found me. My missionary told me his mission was accomplished when he'd found me.

Ironically, this tender moment wound up being one of the most difficult things for me to deal with after joining the Church, because, you see, my missionary literally had finished his mission. It was time for him to go home, which was a difficult thing for me. I felt lost and worried about how I'd go on without my friend to lean on when things got tough.

The night before he went home, I bought pizza and root beer for us to drown our sorrows in. He assured me I would be fine, but I wasn't convinced. I was afraid I'd lose my way without him. He'd taught me so much about the Lord's Church.

In the Baptist church, a pastor is your spiritual guide. He's the one you trust and rely on to lead you down the right path. You build a strong bond with him. This is how I felt about my missionary. He wasn't technically a pastor, but he was my friend and my confidant, and now he was leaving. We said our good-byes, and he gave me his favorite tie to remember him by.

Fast-forward almost twenty years. My son Isaiah wore that very tie when my missionary picked him up from the Salt Lake City Airport and dropped him off at the missionary training center in Provo, Utah, in 2012. Isaiah thought it was pretty cool that my missionary was his companion for a day.

I thought it was pretty cool too.

SECTION II

TO
MORMON
TEACHER

CHAPTER 7

A NEW BEGINNING

L IKE MANY SITUATIONS where people are converted to The Church of Jesus Christ of Latter-day Saints, my family was not happy about my choice to change religions, nor did my mother like the new woman in my life. My mother thought Sebrina forced me to "change gods." In spite of her objections, I knew Sebrina was my soul mate and that our relationship was the start of something beautiful. She was a gift to me from my Heavenly Father, and I was not going to let anyone stand in the way of our happiness.

Sebrina and I were married in a civil ceremony in 1996. We started our lives together with next to no family support, but our love for each other sustained us through those difficult times. We were sealed in the Washington DC Temple on March 28, 1998. The temple is a sacred place in the LDS Church, an edifice that only members who are living up to certain standards can enter. In this building, worthy members perform sacred ordinances that bind families together for eternity, including marriages. This is what Sebrina and I did on that special day. More about this later. (I do tend to get sidetracked, don't I?)

In spite of the beautiful thing Sebrina and I had going, I still had to battle the fallout from my family and old friends. They had long hoped that I would go on to pastor my own church, and maybe even become a TV evangelist. I understood their concerns, but I had a higher power to answer to, and it was His business that I needed to be about. My family and old friends wanted nothing to do with the Mormon life I had chosen or the people that came with it.

Becoming a Mormon was not the easiest thing to do, especially with the same old friends in my life. You see, they didn't want to let go of the old me. They didn't think anything was wrong in my life, and they liked me the way I was. As I tried to grow and improve, my old friends fought the change that facilitated that growth and improvement.

I got to the point where I had to cut them loose so that I could grow into what my Father had called me to do and to become. This was difficult to do. It was like when you lift the lid off a crab basket. When one crab tries to get out, another crab grabs it and pulls it back down.

How can a self-respecting black man become a member of the Mormon Church? How can you change gods just like that? You don't believe in the same Jesus anymore?

These questions and others like them are what my old friends and acquaintances peppered me with. I'm sure other converts have had to undergo this type of treatment from old friends—and probably even family members.

I've read a lot of motivational books and one of the common themes in those books is to stay away from "dream killers." You know, the people who judge, criticize, discourage, and try to stop you from making good things happen in your life. Yep, the ones who "listeth to obey" (Alma 3:27) the wrong source. Most of my family and old friends didn't support my change of life because they didn't understand what I was doing. My family and old friends refused to even investigate the LDS Church to try to understand. They wanted things to stay the way they had been.

Sebrina and I decided to get away from the "dream killers," so we packed our things and moved to Virginia. Upon our arrival, members of our new ward showed up at our home to greet us, help us unpack, and get settled in our new home. It was humbling to see the outpouring of love and support from so many people that we didn't even know. That didn't matter to them; they showed up anyway to make us feel welcome and to help bear our burden.

Not one of those folks left until we were all unpacked! They even ordered pizza! Our new ward family demonstrated the pure love of Christ on our behalf even before we attended our first church meeting with them. Our fellow ward members embraced us as much as the ward members in Ohio had embraced Sebrina. I was blown away.

A lot of our ward members in Virginia were military families, so they were very transient. Because of their military backgrounds, they were racially diverse. We worshipped with people from all around the world in that ward. For instance, the ward's Gospel Principles teacher—Brother Johnson—was part African American, part Japanese. His lessons were powerful and full of conviction. This was still my favorite class to attend; he just made it that much more enjoyable.

I was so impressed by Brother Johnson that I stuck to him like glue. His understanding of the scriptures was amazing. I referred to him as my battle buddy. We use this term in the military for the person of equal rank that is responsible for you, and vice versa. He took me under his wing and was assigned to be my home teacher.

This was all still new to me at the time. Home teaching, visiting teaching, Relief Society, quorums—I've got to admit, I was a bit overwhelmed by it all sometimes. But it was exactly what I needed to help me learn how to help bear other peoples' burdens, just as I had covenanted to do when I was baptized.

My battle buddy and I became close. One night, or should I say morning, he called me and said, "Wain, get your scriptures. You've got to read this!" I grabbed my scriptures and noticed it was 2 a.m. Sebrina was not as excited as my battle buddy and I were, so I got kicked out of bed to take the phone call.

I made it to the kitchen to read the verses with my battle buddy over the phone and cried a lot as the Spirit testified to me, as He had many times before, about the truthfulness of what I had just read. In fact, not only did my battle buddy help me learn a lot from the scriptures, but he was also the one who got me interested in going to the temple. Prior to meeting him, I really didn't give going to the temple much thought.

I'm getting ahead of myself here. Bear with me. I'll fill you in on my path to the temple in a little bit.

The bishop in our new ward wasted no time in getting me ordained to the Aaronic Priesthood. Soon after, he enrolled me in the Melchizedek Priesthood prep classes, where I learned about that priesthood's duties and the authority that came with it.

The Aaronic Priesthood is known as the lesser priesthood, not because its importance is less than the higher priesthood—which is known as the Melchizedek Priesthood—but because its authority and responsibilities are of lesser power. The Aaronic Priesthood is generally held by the younger males, ages 12–17, but is also the priesthood to which male adult converts are ordained shortly after baptism. This was what happened to me. I didn't meet with the teenagers in their quorums; I met in the elders quorum with males more my age. The authority that came with the Aaronic Priesthood was to prepare me for the higher priesthood.

When the Melchizedek Priesthood prep class started, the bishop asked me when I wanted to be ordained to the higher priesthood. I understood that the higher priesthood had a lot more responsibilities, and I was not eager to take them on.

"Hold up, Bishop," I told him. "The Melchizedek Priesthood comes with *way* more responsibility than I can keep up with." I didn't want the responsibility of that much power and authority, not to mention having to account to my Heavenly Father for how I used it.

All the frustrations you've had about blacks not being able to hold the priesthood, and now you don't want to even hold it! Going by the look on his face, I figured this is what the bishop was thinking. He was understanding of my concerns, though, and advised me of the blessings I could bring to my family and others by holding the Melchizedek Priesthood. That didn't matter; I didn't want any part of the Melchizedek Priesthood at that point in my life.

I finished the Melchizedek Priesthood prep class anyway and was then invited to take it again later that year. I agreed but made it clear to the bishop that I was not ready—nor did I think I ever would be—to receive the higher priesthood. I ended up taking that class three times before the stake president got involved. He showed up one Sunday after I became a three-time graduate of the Melchizedek Priesthood prep class—just to speak to me! He took me into the bishop's office to see if he could convince me to receive the priesthood. I told him, like I told the bishop, that I didn't want the responsibility that came with the Melchizedek Priesthood.

Then he said something that shook me to the core. "Brother Myers, not accepting the Melchizedek Priesthood doesn't relieve you of its responsibilities, because you have the knowledge of what it is and the role it should be playing in your life. To be quite honest, you've taken the class three times now, so you know about it better than most!"

They got me—but in a good way!

On January 18, 1998, my battle buddy conferred the Melchizedek Priesthood on me and ordained me to the office of Elder. *Elder Myers!* Not quite, but I felt really good about it. What made it even more satisfying was that my line of authority could be traced directly back to Peter, James, and John, who received it directly from Jesus Christ!

I didn't realize how important this line of authority was until I ordained my son Isaiah an elder before his mission. In spite of my stubborn ways, receiving the Melchizedek Priesthood marked the beginning of the period that has brought the greatest blessings to my family and me.

CHAPTER 8

GOD IS CALLING

MY FIRST CALLING as a member of the LDS Church was as a ward missionary. Every calling in the Lord's Church is important; there are no such things as big or small callings. But to me, my calling as a ward missionary felt special. While it wasn't the same as a full-time missionary's call, it was special to me because it involved teaching the gospel, which I felt was a call my Father issued to me very early in my life.

Holding a calling in the LDS Church took some getting used to because I came from a background in the Baptist and Pentecostal faiths. In these churches, and many others, the more members a preacher attracts, the more popular and important the preacher becomes.

In many other churches, the preacher is the most vital part of that church's success. If he's a skilled preacher, the congregation will grow. If he's not, it won't.

Have you ever seen a church that looks like a rundown and abandoned old house? Have you ever seen one that looks like a grand shopping mall? The difference between these types of churches is the preacher. You can guess which one has a skilled and charismatic preacher. It's sad to say, but in many religions, a preacher makes or breaks the church. This is why they have boards and committees that select new preachers when the need arises. These boards and committees can also pull the plug on a preacher's assignment if the membership decreases too much.

FROM BAPTIST PREACHER TO MORMON TEACHER

It doesn't work that way in the LDS Church. Skilled preacher, teacher, missionary, or not, all are the same in the Lord's eyes. This reality is evident in the Church, and I had to learn a whole different perspective in order to get used to the way things went when it came to serving in a calling.

As a Baptist preacher, I focused on the size of the congregation to determine if I was serving God the right way. It wasn't easy getting over this misconception. In the LDS Church, we want our congregations to grow too, but through different ways and for different reasons.

In my first calling in the LDS Church as a ward missionary, I had to grow and develop into a person who wanted to do the will of God for His children. I needed to learn how to serve my Father's children better—and on a much more personal basis—and to keep their needs as the main reason for my service. This is how the Savior served while He was on the earth, so that is how I needed to learn how to serve. As I learned to serve in this manner, I began to find true joy.

Speaking of joy, I have come to realize that joy is a journey and not a destination. Joy is a choice, not an accident waiting to happen. Joy is a decision we can make at any time and in any situation. Happiness is an emotion that comes and goes. It's a reaction to external events. Joy, however, is a state of mind that comes from within and can be eternal.

While serving as a ward missionary, and in callings that have followed, I gained an eternal perspective for how I should serve my brothers and sisters. I believe this is the perspective that my Father in Heaven wants me—and you—to have.

I've come to love and appreciate the way callings are given and accepted in the LDS Church. I especially love the fact that there are no paid clergy in the Church. Money and the clergy is a topic with which I'm all too familiar. I knew that accepting the world's money for supposedly serving God as a Baptist preacher was wrong, and I still feel strongly about that. We're taught that because we live *in* the world does not mean we have to be *of* the world.

There are many callings in the LDS Church, and each and every one of them has no big *I* and little *you*. No one calling is more important than the other. It may seem that way to some—even some members of the Church—but at the heart of every calling is a mandate to serve and love God's children. In this sense, each calling in the Church is of equal importance.

I've found that the Lord tends to call us to positions within the Church that will open our hearts and stretch us to our limits if we are submissive enough. In other words, when filled with our whole heart and soul, Church callings—no matter which ones—help us become more like our Heavenly Father and His Son.

The calling system in the Church is designed by God and is a perfect system. It's us mortals who imperfectly fill the callings. However, if we accept the callings that come to us and carry them out with all of our hearts, the experiences and blessings we gain will be of great spiritual worth to us—and those whom we serve.

In the years since my baptism, I've served in several callings. I've loved each of them, though some were more difficult to fill than others. The common thread with all the callings I've held in the LDS Church is learning to love those whom I serve. When I do this wholeheartedly, the mechanics of the calling come easier and, in the big picture, are of less importance than the love that binds those who serve and are served.

Before moving to Utah in 2014, I served on my stake's high council in Indiana. I was shocked when the stake president extended this call to me, and I had to ask him if he was sure he was talking to the right person. He assured me that he was and expressed confidence in my ability to serve well in the calling.

After accepting this calling, I realized that I was the only black leader in that stake. Talk about pressure! As I settled into the calling, I learned that high council members are local authorities, similar to how Apostles are to the entire Church. This was not an easy concept for me to wrap my mind around, but once I did, I embraced the calling and served with all of my might, mind, and strength. I loved serving as a member of the stake high council. That doesn't mean there weren't any challenges. In fact, the most difficult part of that calling for me was participating in disciplinary courts, especially when excommunication was involved. These situations were the most difficult for me, but they were also times when I felt closest to my Father in Heaven. It amazed me how such a tough situation like excommunication could be so kind, loving, and beneficial to the person being disciplined. I'd never seen such genuine love and compassion extended by Church leaders to a member of the Church. Truly amazing.

My favorite part of this calling was the speaking assignments. I love speaking in sacrament meeting, and the opportunity to do so came often as a member of the high council. Traveling the country to give talks would be my dream come true!

One time, a sister shouted out "Amen!" while I was speaking in a sacrament meeting. I loved it because it made me feel at home. I said "Amen!" right back at her. I love teaching from the pulpit. To me, it's sacred ground. We'll get more into that later.

Home teaching is another assignment in the Church that has brought me great joy. Home teaching involves a companionship of priesthood holders—usually one Melchizedek Priesthood holder and one Aaronic Priesthood holder—visiting an assigned group of families on at least a monthly basis. The visits consist of small talk and a spiritual message, which typically comes from one of the three highest-ranking living Apostles, including the President of the Church. If performed correctly, this assignment becomes more than just a monthly visit; it becomes a friendship in which the companionship and the family become close to each other. Ideally, the home teachers are the first people a family contacts when help is needed. Good home teachers will be able to see a need and offer help before it's requested.

Home teaching is an assignment with which many in the Church struggle. I won't sugarcoat it; I struggle with this assignment too. I do my home teaching more often than not, but I know I can do better. Once I'm in a family's home, I'm good, but it's making the time and commitment to visit that is difficult.

One of the most difficult things about serving as a home teacher is determining when a family has troubles and needs help. Most peoples' inclination is to say that everything's okay, but sometimes it's not. This is why it's so important for home teachers to be a true friend to the family. A real friend can tell when a family needs a little help.

As bearers of the holy priesthood, we have a lot of room for improvement when it comes to the home teaching program. When we gain the perspective that we are acting for our Father in Heaven and our Savior when home teaching, we cannot fail in this, or any other calling.

CHAPTER 9

PATRIARCHAL BLESSING

W HAT IF YOU could receive a letter from God that provided you with a small glimpse of what He has in store for you in this life and the next? Who wouldn't want such a thing? Hold on to your bowl of cereal—there *is* such a thing! It's called a patriarchal blessing, and it's available to members of the Church through the power of His priesthood.

When I first learned about patriarchal blessings as a new convert, I was amazed. I always knew my Father knew me as an individual, but when I found out He has specific instructions meant for my ears only, I was floored—figuratively, of course, but not by much.

Patriarchal blessings aren't handed out like candy on Halloween night. No, sir. One who receives such a gift must spiritually prepare and be mature enough to receive it. Most members of the Church are in their mid to late teens when they seek this blessing, but some are younger or older. The older adults who seek a patriarchal blessing are typically converts to the Church or members who have come back after a long period of inactivity. I received my patriarchal blessing as an adult because I was a convert.

Like most things involving the Church, I met with my bishop to answer a few questions to make sure I understood what I was seeking. Once the bishop determined I was good to go, I made an appointment with the patriarch, who's been given the priesthood authority and power to give this sacred blessing by placing his hands on my head and speaking on behalf of our Father in Heaven through prayer. Beautiful!

When I went to the patriarch's house for my blessing, I could feel the Spirit the second I walked through the door. While we visited for a bit before the blessing, I could tell this was no ordinary meeting. My patriarch was calm, kind, and inviting. Even though we'd just met, I felt like he knew me. When he laid his hands on my head, the tears began to flow. The words from my Father flowed through the patriarch's mouth and into my ears. It was a blessing like one I'd never had before. I wanted to run and share my gift with the world, but I knew it was meant only for me. Not only did my loving Father in Heaven send His Son to atone for my sins, but He also gave me personal guidance in the form of a patriarchal blessing.

I stand all amazed!

CHAPTER 10

WHEN THE HONEYMOON IS OVER

BECOMING A MEMBER of The Church of Jesus Christ of Latter-day Saints is like all good things—the honeymoon eventually wears off. Everything that seemed so wonderful, exciting, and beautiful lost its shininess and became a challenge, a chore, and, in some ways, a burden.

This post-honeymoon phase is a sensitive subject, but it's also a vital phase that will either make a convert stronger or break him down into falling away from the Church. After I'd been a member of the Church for a few years, I was still dealing with so many different spiritual emotions that at times I felt spiritually and physically drained. That was when it seemed Satan's attacks were the strongest. I've seen a lot of new members start out with strong and vibrant testimonies, only to see the flame of their testimonies wither and die during this post-honeymoon phase.

So how did I survive this phase? Let me tell you, it wasn't easy, and it certainly wasn't without a fair share of mistakes.

Our time in Virginia was wonderful, and our family thrived spiritually. My battle buddy and home teaching companion, Brother Johnson, and I got along well, and we loved the members of our ward.

Shortly after I received the Melchizedek Priesthood, our bishop began talking to Sebrina and me about going to the temple. I really had no knowledge about the importance of the temple at the time, nor did I have any clue about the blessings my Father had in store in the temple for my sweetheart and me. So when the bishop talked to us about attending the temple, my desire to go was missing in action.

You see, I had already entered the post-honeymoon phase and was struggling—more like not even wanting—to progress. Thankfully, we were part of a ward that knew how to show love and support in all things. This was the case with our going to the temple too. Their concern and love was well intentioned, but it sure came across as pushy. Yeah, I said it. *Pushy.*

In my mind, I had received all the blessings I could handle at the time. I belonged to the Lord's true Church, which He led me to like He promised. I held the Melchizedek Priesthood and was trying, though not always successfully, to live up to its responsibilities. So why were so many members trying to push my wife and me to the temple?

I've come to learn over the years that seasoned members of the LDS Church have much more knowledge of the gospel and its many blessings than converts do. Much like I imagine our Heavenly Father feels, they're eager for converts to receive all the blessings that Father has in store for them. Though members at times may seem pushy—*and they are!*—their pushiness comes from a good place and in a loving way. They're pushing converts toward where Father's richest blessings are found. In spite of all of the ward members' good intentions, their pushing me in the direction of the temple was hard to endure.

I remember when Brother Johnson and his wife stopped by our house for a visit. He had a tag from his T-shirt sticking out, and his wife attempted to fix it. His somewhat annoyed reaction was uncomfortable to us all as he asked her to stop pulling on his shirt. She told him that his tag was sticking out, to which he replied that she could wait to fix it in private. As they discussed the matter, my curiosity about garments grew.

I didn't know much about the temple garment back then, so I asked my battle buddy about them. I learned that the garment, in simple terms, is sacred underwear. Once worthy members of the Church go to the temple for the first time, they are to wear the garments at all times, within reason. The garments are sacred to those who go to the temple, so in a way, I kind of understood his irritation. They serve as reminders of the covenants one makes in the temple.

This was one of those key conversations that led to deeper discussions about the temple. I don't remember exactly how the conversations went down, but I do remember the feelings the conversations stirred within me. The Spirit was so strong while we spoke of the temple, and then it happened—my heart fluttered. With the fluttering came a sense of happiness and a strong desire to attend the temple.

Our Father in Heaven has a perfect plan for each of us, I have no doubt about that. What's even more beautiful is that He uses His children to help each other along the path He has designed for us. Had it not been for a loving home teacher, I'm not sure I would've ever found the desire to go to the temple!

I've learned over the years that when I have no desire to move forward in the gospel, and my pushy brothers and sisters in Christ try to move me forward, I should close my eyes, take a deep breath, and trust in my Father.

So what should converts do when the honeymoon of joining the Church is over? Muster all your faith together, and trust in God. Easier said than done, I know, but it really boils down to this formula.

HEAVENLY FATHER'S DAUGHTERS seem to understand spiritual things more quickly than His hardheaded, stubborn sons. My wife, Sebrina, had a desire to go to the temple long before I desired to go, so you can imagine how happy she was to see that I'd *finally* caught up to her.

Going to the temple for the first time, like all big life events, involves preparation. The Church offers a class that prepares first-time temple goers for this big step. The students learn important things about the temple, such as what to expect in the temple and the importance of what we will learn there. The class takes place over several weeks and ends just prior to going to the temple for the first time.

FROM BAPTIST PREACHER TO MORMON TEACHER

We asked my battle buddy and his wife to be our escorts for our first trip to the temple. An escort is someone who acts as your guide on your maiden voyage. They gladly accepted.

We decided to make the trip to Kensington, Maryland—where the Washington DC Temple is located—an overnight excursion. Our escorts surprised us by putting us up in a honeymoon suite, complete with sparkling cider and chocolate kisses on the bed. After dinner with our escort couple that night, we took a drive on the belt-way that leads to the temple. As we approached the temple, it looked to me as if the hand of God had reached down to earth and placed the temple in the perfect spot. It was the most breathtakingly beautiful building I'd ever seen.

The next morning, Sebrina and I were a bundle of nerves about the unknown of what would happen in the temple. As we drove up the winding road that led to the temple that special morning, we listened to a children's choir singing "I Feel My Savior's Love," which was appropriate, to say the least. You can imagine our tears of joy when we realized that we'd arrived on holy ground. No crying uncontrollably, no hysterical sobs, just tears of joy silently rolling down our cheeks as we felt the love of our friends, Heavenly Father, and each other. We took a deep breath, reveled in the beauty of the moment, and then entered the Lord's house.

The feelings and sacred memories of that day remain strong with us to this day.

While we were breaking for lunch in the temple, Bishop Weston came strolling in, surprising us all. Bishop Weston was our bishop in Ohio when I was investigating the Church. He'd made the trip just for our sealing! We had no idea how he knew, but it touched us deeply that he cared enough to travel so far for our special occasion.

It was a beautiful way on a beautiful day to begin our eternal companionship.

MY GRANDMOTHER HAD a heart attack shortly after our sealing. She was like a mother to me and was the only one in my family to support my marriage to Sebrina. I wanted to be near my grandmother after she suffered the heart attack, so we decided to move back to Ohio so we could be of service. It was tough leaving the friends we'd made in Virginia, but we felt it was what we should do.

When we returned to Ohio, I began struggling with some of the old questions and problems I had when I was investigating the Church. I started losing my desire to go to church at all. I found excuses to miss my church meetings. My only saving grace was that we continued praying as a family morning and night, continued studying the scriptures together, and continued holding weekly family home evening.

DURING THIS PHASE when I stopped going to church, I invited the elders quorum members to our home for a game of dominoes. The second counselor in the bishopric joined us, though I doubted he was any match for my mad domino skills. We had a good relationship, and I felt like I could talk to him about anything. I opened up to him about the things I was struggling with and how I was no longer feeling the Spirit like I did when I first joined the Church. I told him that when I went to church, I needed to be spiritually fed. I was starving for someone to preach the inspiring word of God to me, and I wasn't getting that at church.

In yet another moment when my Father spoke to me through another of His children, that bishopric member took a deep breath and said something that has stuck with me ever since. "Wain, you've been feeling and feasting upon all the wonders of the Spirit that God has given *them* to share with *you*. Now it's time to start sharing with others all the wonders of the Spirit that God has given *you* to share with *us*."

I'd never looked at it like that before. Talk about an about-face! There I was, gladly receiving from others and never thinking to give back. I felt I had nothing to offer the people who seemed to have everything in that ward.

Did he say they need me? A black man from nowhere whose father abandoned him, whose mother forsook him, whose teachers figured he would never amount to anything, and who has nothing? The members of this ward need the gifts of the Spirit my Father had given me?

Wow! This was hard for me to comprehend.

From that night on, no matter what I faced at church or in my life, I clung hard to this new perspective. Not only could I endure anything, but I also had gifts my Father had given me to share with my brothers and sisters, even though outwardly they seemed to have it all.

I came to realize that one of these gifts was love for my fellow man, even when I felt they treated my family and me poorly. For instance, when my kids came home from church crying because Primary kids refused to play with them because they were black, I had a gift from my Father to help those Primary children and their families understand us better by showing love to them. Sebrina and I made it a point to visit those families when those instances arose and not to take offense. In our visits, we taught them about who we are and who God chose us to be.

On another occasion, my son Isaiah came to me in tears after being scolded by an elder for cutting through the cultural hall. As father and son, we went to that elder in the spirit of love and spoke to him about the incident. He apologized to Isaiah, who later told me he was scared to approach the man. Because of the incident and the spiritual gifts Father had given me, I was able to help my son learn how to face his fears and to stand up and be a man of God at all times and in all places.

So what should a new member of the Church do when the honeymoon is over? You refuse to let it end! You find a way to keep the fire burning.

In my walk with Christ, I've learned that my relationship with Him is like any other relationship. I need to nourish it with love and affection, nurture it with my time and attention.

In my relationship with my sweet Sebrina, I try to learn new things about her daily. We talk all the time and openly share our affection. This keeps our marriage fresh, new, and full of love and life!

And so it is in our relationship with Jesus Christ and His Church. If we don't want the honeymoon to end, then we need find a way to continually fall in love with Him and His Church. We need to work at building an eternal relationship with Him. We need to keep praying and seeking His influence. I promise you that if you endure all things lovingly and patiently while being obedient to His commandments, He'll show up in all that you do and say to help fire up your testimony.

The honeymoon doesn't have to end, and it never will if you do these things.

CHAPTER 11

WOLVES IN SHEEP'S CLOTHING

As members of The Church of Jesus Christ of Latter-day Saints, we endure more than our fair share of hatred, criticism, and judgment. This became evident to me when I started opening up and sharing my beliefs on my blog and elsewhere. I can usually handle these types of attacks on my religion, but there's been a few times that it was difficult for me to deal with what are known as anti-Mormon sentiments and attacks.

I first encountered anti-Mormon literature a few months after I joined the Church. It was a hot summer day in Ohio, so I left the windows cracked a little to keep the temperature down in the car for when we returned after church services. After church, I noticed a small pamphlet had been slipped through the cracked window onto the car's front seat. The pamphlet had a picture of Jesus on it with the head hollowed out.

Let me take a moment to say I've been a member of several churches over the years, and until that Ohio summer day, I'd never seen a situation where someone went out of their way to go to a church with the sole intent of openly attacking that church's beliefs. It boggled my mind! I could feel the hatred and bitterness through that pamphlet, and I felt bad for whoever felt the need to do this.

While some fellow LDS members get all riled up and angry over these attacks, I see them as confirmations that the LDS Church really is the Lord's true Church. The pamphlet—and all of the anti-Mormon situations I've come across since—bothered me, but I knew that to be like my Savior, I had to endure some of what He endured—on a much smaller scale, of course.

Another anti-Mormon experience happened while we were living in Virginia. I got home from work, checked the mailbox, and found a small packet that looked like a community newsletter. I didn't give it much thought and put it on the mail table for my wife to deal with. You know how it is, husbands, if it's not a check or doesn't look like a check, we aren't too eager to deal with it.

Eventually, Sebrina got to the mail and started reading the "news-letter," which contained information accusing the LDS Church of being a cult and exposed controversial aspects of its history. We were well aware of the controversial aspects by then, so we didn't give the document much thought. It still bothered me, though. Someone going out of their way to deliberately tear down the beliefs of some-one's church was beyond my comprehension.

It's interesting how anti-Mormons throw the word *cult* around to hurt and intimidate members of the LDS Church. It's as if they think that one word and all it entails is going to dissuade us from believing the Church's teachings. Sadly, I guess it does work on some members. I've been blessed enough to see this nasty, ugly practice for what it is: more of Satan's lies and tools of deception.

Of all the run-ins I've had with anti-Mormons since I joined the Church in 1995, a recent one was the worst I've encountered. It came shortly after I started posting my life's experiences on my blog. Interestingly, the entire conversation took place through Facebook's Instant Messenger app. Check it out:

> IM: *Hello, how are you?*
>
> Me: *I'm well, thanks! And you?*
>
> IM: *Good, thanks. This winter has been a cold one.*
>
> Me: *Very cold! To what do I owe the pleasure of this conversation?*

The person's name looked familiar, so I went back through the comments on my blog and noticed this person had made a com-ment in response to one of my posts. It was evident he was looking for a fight. I didn't respond to his comment on my blog because I figured it was a public forum, which is not the place for us to debate. I thought my lack of response to his comment was why he decided to reach out to me via Facebook.

IM: *I was just wondering if you're aware that the Book of Mormon teaches that the white race is superior and the Indians and black people are "cursed" by God with a dark skin.*

Me: *I'm aware that's one of the interpretations.*

IM: *(after providing links to a couple of anti-Mormon websites) I'm afraid it's more than interpretation; it's what leaders of your church taught. "Shall I tell you the law of God in regard to the African race? If a white man who belongs to the chosen seed mixes his blood with the seed of Cain, the penalty, under the law of God, is death on the spot. This will always be so" (Brigham Young, Journal of Discourses, Volume 10, page 110).*

Me: *First off, let me thank you for leaving the ninety and nine to reach out to the one you believe is lost, just as Christ taught.*

IM: *LDS's "God" is truly nothing like the God of the Bible, and their gospel of handshakes and progression are not the good news of Christianity.*

This guy went all over the place, as you will see.

Me: *After we review the information you provided with an open heart, [IM], are you willing to do the same? Also, if I may ask, what is your race? Your first question accuses the Book of Mormon of teaching this curse, and then you refer to a quote by Brigham Young. So let me ask you, are you accusing the Book of Mormon or Brigham Young—a white man that was a prophet and also a product of his time and society—for teaching this curse?*

This is where "IM" took a turn for the worse.

IM: *Sorry! I'm white and am a former member of the Church living in western New York. I'm now a Christian after studying the New Testament.*

Me: *Oh okay! Just curious. Is this the reason you left the Church? And were you a convert or born into the Church? And what are you sorry about?*

IM: *If members of the Church don't pay a full tithe, they will not be able to get into the LDS temple in order to receive their endowment and get sealed, and ultimately be able to be with God the Father. There is a cost to it. It's a requirement to be with God. Do you see my point? For Christians outside your faith, it's a free gift, His gift to us. It's grace through our faith. Through this, we are with God the Father. We then give to help churches, widows, and the homeless because "faith works." Hope this makes sense. When Jesus died, the veil of the temple was rent. I know it was Him who set me free from Mormonism. I can't help but be a Christian for this reason.*

Me: *Okay, so tithing was the reason you left? Or was it not being able to go into the house of the Lord without being obedient to His word?*

IM: *You need to open your eyes, my friend, and see the simple truth of the gospel. It's not "saved by grace after all you can do," it's saved by grace, not works (Ephesians 2:8–9), and justified by faith, not works (Galatians 2:15–16). It's the mercy of God that saves us, not our righteous acts (Titus 3:5). It's because we are saved and have true faith that the fruit of faith, good works, comes from us (James 2:14–26). Alma in the Book of Mormon teaches that God can't save us in our sins, but Romans 5:8–10 teaches that even while we were sinners (IN our sin) and enemies to God, Christ died for us! That is the good news, and I pray that you will accept it before it's too late.*

If you think this post was long, you should see the other four in which he goes on and on, ranting and quoting scriptures that, in his mind, prove Mormonism to be wrong! I've spared you from the monotony of reading them. You're welcome.

Me: *I can feel your plea, and I understand your purpose. As a former member, you have to know that we live the higher, celestial law. I have found that when a person leaves the LDS*

Church, it's for a personal reason that generally has nothing to do with doctrine. So, I ask you again, why did you leave the LDS Church?

IM: *I left because of the Bible.*

Me: *Were you a convert or born into the Church?*

IM: *Christianity.*

Me: *??? Were you ever really LDS, or are you just trying to pose as a former member? I'm asking because it seems you didn't understand my question. Sometimes people pose as former members to make their point seem valid. If that's the case, we are starting this relationship on the wrong foot. Shall we start over? You don't have to pose as a former member. We can still have an open and honest conversation about the gospel as the person you really are, not as a person that left the LDS Church because of the Bible. I'd like to talk to the real "IM"! Continuing to pose is really not Christlike. In fact, it's like a wolf in sheep's clothing.*

IM: *To Christians, Jesus's death was enough. There is no need to be climbing an exaltation ladder.*

Say what? I was willing to give him the benefit of the doubt, thinking that maybe he didn't read my prior post. Then again . . .

IM: *Jesus died on the cross, the cross which you will never see anywhere in an LDS church. When He died on it, the veil of the temple was rent. I know it was Jesus Christ who came to fulfill the laws and set everybody free. I know it was Him who set me free from Mormonism. I'm a Christian for this reason. You have deviated from what the word of God actually teaches. You have embraced a religion that is nothing more than a collection of cultivated lies by Joseph Smith.*

Me: *The Spirit has revealed to me that you were never a member of the LDS Church. You are trying to enter my life through a closed window, much like a thief or how an enemy would. There is a door to my house. If you wish to enter and have an honest conversation, you must come as you are, not like an enemy! I saw your previous comment on my blog, and I know you're trying to bait me into an argument! How can you profess Christ through a lying tongue? You started this conversation with a lie. So why would I listen to anything else you have to say?*

His next response was the last straw.

    IM: *It's a Christian's duty to witness to Jehovah's Witnesses and LDS.*

So, it was his Christian duty to lie. Wow! It's like an apostate Christian who says, "I can sin, as long as I do it in the name of Jesus Christ. That way, it'll all be forgiven, no matter what I do!"

This seems exactly what "IM" was doing via Facebook. Most anti-Mormons I've come across use similar tactics. How can they expect to bring souls unto Christ using these cunning, deceitful, and just plain un-Christlike methods? And to have the audacity to tell me that if I don't believe what he believes, then I'm going to hell?

"A prudent man concealeth knowledge: but the heart of fools proclaimeth foolishness" (Proverbs 12:23).

———————◆———————

FOR SOME REASON, anti-Mormons think we LDS Church members don't know our history or Church doctrine. They seem to think we've been hit over the head with a "Mormon stick" and dragged into the waters of baptism. They also seem to think that we blindly follow without thought or question.

News flash! One of the main reasons I joined the Church was because I had questions, did my research, and found the answers! I am well aware of how some LDS Church leaders treated black people in the past. I've been a member of the Church since 1995 and have preached the gospel in one capacity or another ever since. I'm well aware of what some of our past leaders said and thought about black folks. Members of the LDS Church are some of the most intelligent people on the earth today. We know our Church history and, in most cases, know it better than anti-Mormons know it.

Anti-Mormons intimidate many members of the LDS Church, and understandably so. If only Latter-day Saints would learn to rely on the Light of Christ at all times and in all places, we'd be better able to deal with anti-Mormon attacks. When the Lord is our guide and our driving influence, we can act with confidence and with boldness, but not be overbearing. As the Lord Himself said, "I am the light which shineth in darkness, and the darkness comprehendeth it not" (D&C 10:58).

Jesus Christ was no coward, nor should we be cowardly. God's word tells us that if we are prepared, we shall not fear (see D&C 38:30). How do we prepare? Feast on and search the scriptures. Pray with real intent. Do what He's asked you to do. Become familiar with the Spirit's guidance. Walk in faith. When we do these things, we *will* be better prepared to deal with anything the devil throws our way, especially the lies the anti-Mormons hurl at us.

I am not ashamed of the gospel of Jesus Christ, nor am I afraid of what anti-Mormons might say or think, because through the power of God, we can overcome all things.

CHAPTER 12

BLACKS AND THE PRIESTHOOD

N ow is as good a time as any to explain how I came to peace with the blacks and the priesthood issue I struggled with when I was investigating the LDS Church.

Prior to June 8, 1978, black men were not allowed to hold the priesthood in the Church. I'm often asked how I came to accept this historical scar that still stirs up anti-Mormon sentiment many years after the revelation that corrected the matter.

Truthfully, I haven't accepted it, and really I don't think I want to. Let me elaborate on this statement.

My wife and I have never been called to serve a full-time or part-time mission for the Church, but we've had plenty of missionary opportunities based solely on the fact that we are people of color. We've lived on the East Coast of the United States and in the Midwest, and we currently reside in Utah. Our travels have given us the chance to meet a lot of people—both LDS and non-LDS. In almost every ward we've been members of, we were the only black family in the ward.

In our travels, we've been blessed to get all the questions you can imagine about black people. *How do blacks view the Church? Do you think black people are cursed? Why do all black people dance so well? Can I touch your hair?* And my personal favorite: *How can any self-respecting black man join the LDS Church, knowing how its leaders feel about black people?*

One of the best things that happened to me while I was trying to find my Father's straight and narrow path was that my faith in men of God was shattered. It didn't feel amazing at the time, but now that I look back, it was nothing but amazing. You see, as I sought counsel from preacher after preacher and received heartbreaking answer after heartbreaking answer, I realized that I was looking for God in all the wrong places. It became painfully evident that I wasn't going to find Him, the real Him, in any of the churches or pastors I was interacting with.

When I found the truth in the LDS Church, I didn't see its leaders as men of God; I saw them as mortal men searching for answers—just like I was. That's not to say that they weren't men of God; that's just to say that I didn't expect them to be perfect. I knew that only one man has walked the earth in perfection. I have a clear understanding that we are all prone to mistakes and bad decisions—even Church leaders.

When Sebrina first told me about the priesthood ban for black men, I was disappointed most in God. I wondered how He could allow this policy to be enforced for so long. The Creator of all mankind withheld the blessings of the priesthood from some of His children because of the color of their skin? My missionary, the one who first taught me, even went to the scriptures and showed me in black and white print that God *cursed* me with black skin.

This fact drove me to my knees, and with tears in my eyes, I felt God speak to my heart and assure me that in due time He would explain the priesthood ban to me. I needed to learn more things before He would bless me with this understanding. If I trusted Him, He would answer all of my questions about this sensitive matter.

One of the first answers He led me to was a quote from Bruce R. McConkie:

> Forget everything that I have said, or what President Brigham Young or President George Q. Cannon or whomsoever [*sic*] has said in days past that is contrary to the present revelation [regarding the priesthood ban]. We spoke with a limited understanding and without the light and knowledge that now has come into the world.
>
> We get our truth and our light line upon line and precept upon precept. We have now had added a new flood of intelligence and light

on this particular subject, and it erases all the darkness and all the views and all the thoughts of the past. They don't matter any more. ("All Are Alike unto God," *BYU Speeches*, CES Religious Educators Symposium address, August 18, 1978)

When Joseph Smith lost the 116 manuscript pages while translating the Book of Mormon, the Lord chastened him:

And behold, how oft you have transgressed the commandments and the laws of God, and have gone on in the persuasions of men.

For, behold, you should not have feared man more than God. Although men set at naught the counsels of God, and despise his words—

Yet you should have been faithful; and he would have extended his arm and supported you against all the fiery darts of the adversary; and he would have been with you in every time of trouble.

Behold, thou art Joseph, and thou wast chosen to do the work of the Lord, but because of transgression, if thou art not aware thou wilt fall.

But remember, God is merciful; therefore, repent of that which thou hast done which is contrary to the commandment which I gave you, and thou art still chosen, and art again called to the work;

Except thou do this, thou shalt be delivered up and become as other men, and have no more gift. (D&C 3:6–11)

I don't think God chose Joseph because he was perfect. I think God chose and called Joseph because of his faith.

When I joined the LDS Church, I had faith in God, not man. This doesn't mean that I don't follow the President of the Church and sustain him and the First Presidency and Quorum of the Twelve Apostles as prophets, seers, and revelators. I do, however, realize that they are mortal men prone to make mistakes, just like all of us are. If they make mistakes and speak as mortal men, I'm not going to lose my faith in God the Father over it. Nor will my faith be shattered or my heart be broken. We've all made mistakes and fallen short of perfection, and I don't think the prophets are exempt from those same weaknesses.

God uses flawed men to do His perfect work. This fact is one of the most amazing things about my Father in Heaven, and it gives me hope that in spite of our mortal weaknesses, the gospel of Jesus Christ will go forward—as it has already!

Elder Jeffrey R. Holland said in his April 2013 general conference talk "Lord, I Believe," "Except in the case of His only perfect Begotten Son, imperfect people are all God has ever had to work with. That must be terribly frustrating to Him, but He deals with it. So should we. And when you see imperfection, remember that the limitation is not in the divinity of the work" (*Ensign*, May 2013).

When people ask me how I got over the pain I felt about the priesthood ban, I tell them that I haven't yet—and hope I never will. This pain and confusion fuel my testimony and further solidify my knowledge that God is great and that His work will go forth no matter the weaknesses of mortal man.

This understanding and point of view are what make my testimony strong. My testimony has been tested time and again. I share my testimony whenever I can and with whoever will listen. My testimony has been challenged and treated with disrespect by unbelievers more often than it's been accepted. Each time I'm challenged, I study and learn something new about my Father and His Son's Church.

CHAPTER 13

TESTIMONY AND TESTIFYING

S OME PEOPLES' TESTIMONIES are tender because they haven't been tried in the crucible of fire and adversity. Testimonies should be tried and tested, because that's how we grow them and increase in our conviction that the gospel is true. When our testimony grows and we're being true to the faith, we become more sensitive to the promptings of the Holy Ghost.

When we strengthen our testimony, the Lord will inspire us to act and will call upon us to open our mouths and preach His word. Here are a few examples of how these truths have played a part in my life as a Mormon teacher.

I'm a fan of gospel hip-hop music. The tunes in my car often arrive at my destination before I do because I enjoy loud music that teaches about Jesus Christ. Like my testimony, I'm not shy about sharing my music.

One evening my boys and I were taking a vacuum cleaner to the missionaries assigned to labor in our area so they could clean their apartment. We were bumping the Christian hip-hop group Crossmovement as we pulled into the apartment parking lot. A group of young men were standing by watching us as we got out of the truck. One of the young men yelled in my direction, asking what I knew about Crossmovement.

"Bruh," I shouted back, "I bump Crossmovement all day!"

He smiled, and we gave each other "the nod." This is how we black men give each other a sign of approval and is our way of saying to each another that we agree or like what's being done. It's the real-world equivalent to "liking" something on Facebook.

We delivered the vacuum, and when we returned to my truck, my "nod" brutha motioned to me that he wanted to talk. He came closer and asked about my visit to the missionaries' apartment. He looked confused as I explained to him why we were there. I mentioned my membership in the LDS Church and bore my testimony to him and the other young men who had gathered around us. The young men, as it turned out, belonged to a popular TV evangelist's congregation that also ran a popular Bible college. I remembered the evangelist because he was one of the preachers I aspired to be like when I was younger, and at one point, I wanted to attend his Bible college.

After I bore my testimony to the young men, my "nod" buddy gave me every reason he could think of as to why the LDS Church was a cult and why I, as a black man, was being deceived and lead astray by Satan. I calmly listened to him. He even went so far as to touch my abdomen in a gesture telling me that the burning in my bosom was a lie from the pits of hell.

When he ran out of ammo, I calmly told him, "You asked me a question, and when I gave you an answer, you went off on me! Which of us is acting more Christlike, you or me?" I told him that if I'd had any doubt about joining the LDS Church before, he just confirmed that I'd made the right decision *to* join the Church.

He tried to continue with his ranting against the Church, but I pointed out that using a combative approach will never work and that it goes contrary to God's commandments. By then, the elders had joined us. I suggested to my young friend that he start using the spirit of love and peace with all men and to open his heart so that the Spirit could move freely from heart to heart. When we finished speaking with each other, we shook hands and agreed to disagree as brothers.

The elders looked on in amazement. Our small crowd dispersed. The elders said they'd been trying to find a way to talk to the young men for a long time. They were convinced the Lord sent me with the vacuum as an answer to their prayers. The elders sent me frequent updates about the success they were having in communicating with those young men after our parking lot discussion.

I don't know if anything came of the conversation, but I do know that because of the confrontational manner in which that young man attacked my beliefs, my testimony grew stronger because I stood firm in the face of opposition and gave heed to the promptings of the Spirit to remain calm and speak boldly of what I knew to be true. Once the Spirit remained involved, all in the vicinity couldn't help but be affected for good.

◇

ON ANOTHER OCCASION, I was out of town on business when the Lord told me to go to the local LDS meetinghouse and introduce myself to the bishop. I did as I was told and introduced myself to the bishop and bore my testimony to him. I could tell he was a little surprised. (I guess I can't blame him. A stranger wanders into his office and bears his testimony. That doesn't happen every day!) I shared my background with him and explained that I felt inspired to help with the missionary work in his ward. He asked for my bishop's contact information and said he'd be in touch if he needed me.

Poor man. Must've thought I was crazy. It's a good thing he talked to our Father about the seemingly random encounter.

I didn't hear from him that week, but the senior missionaries serving in the area contacted me the following weekend and asked if I was still interested in helping with missionary work. I said I was still interested but that I wouldn't be back in that town until the following week. We set a time and place to meet, and they told me how glad they were to meet a former Baptist preacher. They had an investigator whose questions nobody had been able to answer to his satisfaction.

We met the following week at their apartment, and they filled me in on the investigator we were going to meet with that night. The visit involved a part-member family. The wife was a member of the Church, but her husband was not. In fact, he was a Baptist preacher who had some deep questions that the elders couldn't answer, which is why the senior couple got involved.

You know how it is. When the young uns can't handle the situation, they call in the veterans!

When the bishop told the senior couple about my visit and background, they hoped I'd be able to help.

We got to our appointment and made the usual small talk. I could tell the husband was sizing me up. I felt it was time to talk to my new friend—preacher to preacher. I dived in and asked him straight up what questions he had about the Church that nobody could answer. He folded his arms and asked if I'd seen the painting in LDS chapels of the boy Joseph on his knees, leaning back as he looked up at God the Father and His Son. I acknowledged that I had and knew precisely the painting he was talking about. He referred to a verse in the Bible that said no man could see God in the flesh and live, which to him meant that what happened in the painting couldn't be true.

We locked on to each other's eyes, and the Spirit was abundantly present. The senior couple and the preacher's wife looked on as if they were at a tennis match—back and forth, back and forth.

I repeated the preacher's concerns to make sure I understood him correctly. "That's what I'm saying!" he exclaimed. After a brief pause, I asked him which member of the Church told him Joseph remained in the flesh during the experience.

The missionaries' jaws dropped, and the preacher's condescending smirk quickly faded into a look of confusion as he searched for an answer. He slowly smiled and nodded his head several times as he realized nobody had ever told him any such thing.

I pointed out that there's no reference as to whether Joseph remained in the flesh when God the Father and Jesus Christ appeared to him. And if the scripture he referred to earlier was true—and we both believed it was—then Joseph *couldn't* have been in the flesh during the First Vision. My Baptist preacher friend nodded as he realized that he'd answered his own question.

The senior couple was in awe as they shared with me later how strongly they'd felt the Spirit that night. It's such a good feeling when the Lord uses you as a tool to teach His children.

Unfortunately, I—like a lot of full-time missionaries experience—never heard about what became of the investigator, but I know that his heart was touched by our encounter. I hope the seed we planted that night comes into full bloom some day.

WHILE IN COLORADO on business, I attended sacrament meeting at the ward near my hotel. This is where I met the Pinckney family, who invited me to their home for a Sabbath dinner. (You've got to love people who reach out to others, especially total strangers!) I accepted the invitation, and we got to know each other better when I arrived at their home.

Their three-year-old daughter brought me a set of keys while the family finished preparing the meal. I thought it was her way of playing, so I gave the keys back to her and told her to give them to her daddy. Brother Pinckney came back into the living room and told me he knew I needed transportation and that he wanted me to use his car while I was in town. I politely refused, saying I could get anywhere I needed on the hotel shuttle.

As you might have guessed, I wound up driving myself back to the hotel in one of the Pinckney family cars later that evening.

That dinner was the first of several I enjoyed in the Pinckney home on that business trip. One of those meals was a barbecue that the full-time missionaries attended. The elders, as they're prone to do, invited anyone who could to join them to help teach a lesson that night. Nobody accepted and, because I was from out of town, I didn't think the invitation was intended for me.

The missionaries left, and an hour later, they called Brother Pinckney informing him they hadn't found anyone to join them. Brother Pinckney asked if I'd be willing to go with them. The Spirit pricked my heart, and I knew what I needed to do. I picked the elders up, and as I did so, I realized why the Lord had prompted the Pinckneys to offer me their car.

The elders let me know that we were going to visit a part-member family and that it was the husband—who was black—that was the nonmember. He had questions about the Church and didn't totally trust the missionaries' answers. The elders were hesitant to ask my help initially because they figured that it would be an imposition because I was in town on business. Silly elders. Little did they know that I'm *always* on a mission from God!

When we arrived at the appointment, the husband seemed happy to meet with us, but I could tell something was bothering him. Like I'm known to do, I jumped in feet first and cut to the chase. I told him the missionaries informed me that he had a question about the Church that they couldn't answer adequately.

He was just as direct with me. "Why couldn't black men hold the priesthood?" he asked.

I told him what I knew about the ban, including that it was never officially Church doctrine and that God had never given revelation to any prophet for the ban in the first place. It was a practice started by Brigham Young after Joseph Smith died. I told him that the Church was under a lot of pressure at the time and that Brigham Young saw the need to grow the Church. In order to do this, he felt the need to join the white mentality that was dominant in the society at the time. This decision gave birth to the priesthood ban.

I've done a lot of research on this matter over the years, and I've never found anything definitive about when this practice of keeping the priesthood from black men began, I told my new friend. The closest thing I've found in regard to this is that Brigham Young wouldn't allow Elijah Abel, a black Melchizedek Priesthood holder, to receive his temple ordinances in Nauvoo, Illinois.

I could tell the light was coming on in the husband's mind, but his heart wasn't ready to accept the answers yet. So he moved on to deeper doctrinal questions, such as if God really lives on a planet called Kolob.

The couple had a newborn baby boy, so I asked the husband if he loved his son, to which he replied with an emphatic, "Of course I do!"

It was evident that the husband's question about Kolob was well beyond his ability to understand and wasn't immediately relevant to his salvation. So I continued with my line of questioning.

"Would you sit your son down at the dinner table right now and try to feed him all the food he'll need for the rest of his life at once, so you wouldn't need to worry about feeding him again?"

"There's no way he could eat it all," he replied.

"Precisely!" I explained that it was absurd to consider such a thing because it's obvious that humans need to eat a little, sleep a little, and grow a little over time. Our Father in Heaven, I explained, uses the same formula with our spiritual growth. There's no way he—the husband—could digest the answers to the deep questions he was asking without eating a little, pondering a little, and growing a little. This is how Father will feed you His knowledge, I promised him.

He didn't accept the gospel that night, but I could tell that what the Spirit had taught him through me and the missionaries had a powerful effect on him. The elders were impressed with the approach I took in trying to answer the husband's questions and asked for tips on how they could answer particular questions with him in the future. Our visit that night was the beginning of something special for that family.

I returned home shortly after that trip to Colorado with a new-found desire to teach every missionary how to answer the hard questions about the gospel. As God's love would have it, I was called as ward mission leader not long after. Let the classes begin!

About six months later, I received a text message from the wife inviting me back to Colorado to attend her husband's baptism.

Wow! Ain't God good?

———————◇———————

I CLAIM NO credit for my own abilities and skills in these examples. All such glory goes to my Father. I do recognize, however, that because I regularly put forth the effort to read the scriptures, fast, pray, and do the things my Father expects of me that I am better prepared to serve as a tool in His hands. My testimony is also refined and nourished, preparing it better for when the devil and his minions attack.

Think of your testimony as a hot air balloon and faith-building actions—such as scripture study, temple attendance, praying, serving, fasting—as the fire needed to keep it afloat. You can strengthen your testimony so that it will serve you well in times of need and trial. If you've seen a hot air balloon in action, the pilot is constantly feeding fire into the balloon to keep it afloat. Such is the way for you to keep your testimony afloat. Lots of fire! The Spirit of God like a fire is burning! Can I get an "Amen!" up in here?

CHAPTER 14

LIKE A FIRE IS BURNING

AS YOU REMEMBER from the beginning of this book, God called me to preach His word at an early age. That calling is still in effect today, as has been evidenced by the teaching-based callings I've held in the LDS Church. The principles I've come to know and embrace in my life have added to who God created me to be. My greatest joy comes from teaching the gospel of Jesus Christ, but in order for me to best do that, I've learned that I need to meet some prerequisites first.

The Doctrine and Covenants instructs, "Seek not to declare my word, but first seek to obtain my word, and then shall your tongue be loosed; then, if you desire, you shall have my Spirit and my word, yea, the power of God unto the convincing of men" (D&C 11:21).

A teacher's desire should be to please God first if he or she is going to effectively edify others through the Holy Ghost. God's words have to be etched upon the teacher's heart through regular study and prayer in order to be an effective tool in the Lord's hands.

In the Book of Mormon, we read about some well-prepared teachers:

> Now these sons of Mosiah were with Alma at the time the angel first appeared unto him; therefore Alma did rejoice exceedingly to see his brethren; and what added more to his joy, they were still his brethren in the Lord; yea, and they had waxed strong in the knowledge of the truth; for they were men of a sound understanding and they had

searched the scriptures diligently, that they might know the word of God.

But this is not all; they had given themselves to much prayer, and fasting; therefore they had the spirit of prophecy, and the spirit of revelation, and when they taught, they taught with power and authority of God. (Alma 17:2–3)

As a member of the LDS Church who is often blessed with the opportunity to preach, I pattern my teaching preparation after these words and fine examples. I prepare to teach by studying the scriptures and other preparatory material, and as I have done so, the word of God has come to life and has found a place deep in my heart.

Prayer is a way to seek my Father's counsel by speaking directly to Him. This should be an integral part of any teacher's preparation to teach and preach the gospel. How can I expect to be able to share what He wants me to share unless I talk to Him about it?

Fasting is also a necessary ingredient for spiritual growth and preparation. It's an act of spiritual intimacy that helps my spirit overcome the weaknesses and hungers of the flesh. Fasting helps me feel more and more love for my Father and Savior through the Holy Ghost. It's one of the most personal and sacred acts in my life and is a source of great spiritual strength.

Several LDS Church members and friends have commented that it must have been difficult for me to leave the Baptist church and start all over again in the LDS Church. I don't see it that way. For me, joining the LDS Church didn't make it necessary to start from the beginning. My Father in Heaven knew me before I came to earth, and He led me to the true Church where I could take what He had already given me and add to it.

Since becoming a member of the LDS Church, I've encountered a few cultural differences that took a little adjustment. For example, in the Baptist church, the same preacher delivers the sermon almost every Sunday, so it was strange to me that in the LDS Church we didn't have the same preacher every week. To make things even stranger, it was folks from the congregation that delivered the sermons!

Most people would rather go to the dentist than deliver public speeches. As members of the LDS Church, however, it's our *responsibility* to take our turn to speak in sacrament meeting. This truth makes it imperative for us to take the time to learn how to speak and communicate our thoughts and feelings to a congregation from the pulpit.

The way I see it, there's always somebody in the Church audience that's in need. If this weren't true, nobody would be there in the first place. Every time I've stood at the pulpit to speak—whether as a Baptist preacher or Mormon teacher—I feel the congregation's need. The members *need* me to follow the direction of the Spirit and to speak inspiring words from our Father in Heaven.

Preparing for the sacred responsibility of speaking in sacrament meeting is vital when we accept an invitation from the bishopric to address the ward. Think about it. When you're in the audience, you don't want to sit through a talk where it's obvious the speaker did little to prepare. This is why praying, studying, fasting, and following the Spirit's direction is so important when giving a talk in sacrament meeting.

Another key ingredient when preparing for a speaking assignment is practice, practice, practice! Did I mention you should also practice?

Do you think speakers who deliver a talk with the tongue of angels didn't prepare and practice? I make it a habit to practice giving a talk, even when I don't have an assignment to speak! I practice in the mirror while shaving. I practice in my car while driving. If I have some extra time to kill in the morning, I give a talk.

As I deliver these impromptu talks, I focus on how to communicate my thoughts and on what words are the best to use. When I do have a speaking assignment, the thoughts and words formed in these practice talks serve as the tools the Spirit uses to help me speak God's words to my brothers and sisters.

Simply put, effective speakers *practice.*

I've never met a person who wasn't afraid to speak in public at first. I've never met one who hit a home run with their first talk. We all start out scared, stuttering, and nervous. You know what I'm saying. "Uh, good morning brothers and sisters, uh . . ." Or "Ummm . . . my name is Wain Myers . . ."

FROM BAPTIST PREACHER TO MORMON TEACHER

The difference between a good sacrament meeting speaker and a not-so-good sacrament meeting speaker is practice and perspective. If our perspective is that we have a sacred responsibility to prepare and speak the Lord's word to the congregation—and we practice—we *will* become better speakers with each and every assignment.

The pulpit is a sacred place. As a Baptist preacher, I understood that the people sitting in the pews were in spiritual need. I understood that my role as a preacher was to be a conduit through which the Lord uplifted and edified His children. I admit that many of my motives at the time were less than pure, but that was due largely to a lack of light and knowledge. I always practiced and prepared, no matter what.

Never before has the world been in such need of the gospel of Jesus Christ. Preaching His gospel is a sacred responsibility that we, as members of the Lord's true Church, must be willing and ready to do at all times and in all places. Whether we're at the pulpit delivering a talk in sacrament meeting or taking part in a member-present missionary lesson, we have the sacred responsibility to be prepared to speak up when we're asked to do so, and even when we're not. Basically, we need to be ready to teach the gospel whenever the Spirit moves us to open our mouths.

I've been in the sales profession for more than twenty years, but I've been selling all of my life—just like you have. Thing is, most of us don't realize we've been selling all of our lives.

Zig Ziglar tells us that selling is nothing more than a "transference of feeling" ("The Key to Being a Professional Salesperson," Ziglar. com, http://www.ziglar.com/sales/key-being-professional-salesperson). If we can get the person hearing our message to catch our heartfelt and honest enthusiasm about what we're saying, they're more likely to accept our message. I agree wholeheartedly with this.

It's not just *what* you say that inspires and uplifts people, it's *how* you say what you're saying that makes the message even more powerful. Words are just words, but when you attach them to emotion, you're really conveying a powerful message.

My wife says I'm animated when I speak in sacrament meeting. I call it *expression*. My way of expressing the Lord's message connects me to the congregation. When I feel the Spirit, the congregation will feel Him too. The Spirit uses the expression of emotion to testify of truth. When the congregation and speaker feel the Spirit's influence at the same time, it's then and only then that the Holy Ghost is able to attend to the speaker and congregation's needs as a whole. When the audience and speaker are connected, the speaker feels a deep desire, through the Spirit, to minister to the congregation's need.

When I prepare a talk, I never write out the talk. I'll write out a basic outline of what I want to talk about, but the words the Spirit gives me to speak come from hours of studying, praying, practicing, and fasting. This is one of the many reasons that studying scripture, good books, and general conference talks is so important. The things we study and learn will be the words and impressions the Spirit brings to our minds while we're at the pulpit.

When we look at the pulpit as sacred ground, we'll put more into our preparation for that next speaking assignment. You never know when it's coming, so start preparing today!

CHAPTER 15

LOVE UNDER NEW MANAGEMENT

CHARITY. I LOVE charity, which interestingly is love, the pure love of Christ. I had a "hallelujah" moment involving charity once. It started when I was pondering some of the most common questions I've encountered as a member of the LDS Church: "What do Mormons have to do to get into heaven?" and "What is the biggest difference in the Mormon Church from other churches?"

Let me say a little something about the first question.

Mormons have to do the same thing everybody else has to do to get into heaven. It's silly to think that God would have different requirements based on different denominations. Can you imagine denominational lines at the Pearly Gates?

"Baptists, you get in line over here. Methodists, method your way right over to the line on the left. Pentecostals, you're in the wrong section. Mormons, follow me, please."

It's silly!

As I investigated, joined, and have lived as a member of the LDS Church, I've come to the conclusion that the Church is one of the most misunderstood churches around. Misunderstandings don't change the fact that we're all God's children and that we all have to follow the straight and narrow path laid out in the scriptures.

Back to my "hallelujah" moment.

You know by now that I've been a member of several different churches during my life, most notably the Baptist church. None of the churches I attended has compared to the truth that I've found in the LDS Church. My introduction to the Church wasn't the first time I'd felt my Father's influence in my life, but what I felt when introduced to the gospel was more personal and powerful. It was like meeting up with my dearest friend in His house, where He has the most influence. You might say I'm in love under new management.

In my search for the truth, which I like to refer to as my treasure hunt, each of the churches I attended had different ways of reacting to the Spirit—or what they perceived to be the Spirit.

At the first church I remember attending as a child, when a person felt the Holy Ghost, the ushers formed a circle around the influenced member. It was like they were protecting the worshipper from hurting anyone. All of a sudden, the person under the influence of the Holy Ghost started screaming for no apparent reason.

The only phrase that can accurately sum up how I, as a child, felt about this manifestation of the Holy Ghost is, *This scared the H-E-double-hockey-sticks out of me!* I wanted no part of what I was convinced was the devil or one of his demons taking over my body while under the influence of "the spirit."

This is all I witnessed and knew about the Holy Ghost as a child. The people at that church thought that when the Spirit landed on you, anything could happen, so everyone should just get out of the way!

In my teen years, I attended another church with my mother where you had to "tarry" in order to receive the Holy Ghost. Tarrying involves going to the altar, kneeling, and calling on the name of Jesus Christ as loudly and quickly as you could until the Spirit came to you. The only person around who knew if the Spirit had come upon you was the pastor. In other words, keep yelling and carrying on until the pastor told you the Holy Ghost came to you. This did little to ease my fears about receiving the Holy Ghost.

As I look back on these experiences and consider the things people accuse the LDS Church of, I have to shake my head in astonishment.

I've seen people tarry for the Holy Ghost and then leave the church building and cuss people out with the same mouth they were tarrying with a few minutes earlier.

I saw no clarity or consistency in how the churches I attended helped members receive the Holy Ghost. I knew that the Bible was clear on this topic, though.

> Who, when they were come down, prayed for them, that they might receive the Holy Ghost:
>
> (For as yet he was fallen upon none of them: only they were baptized in the name of the Lord Jesus.)
>
> Then laid they their hands on them, and they received the Holy Ghost.
>
> And when Simon saw that through laying on of the apostles' hands the Holy Ghost was given, he offered them money,
>
> Saying, Give me also this power, that on whomsoever I lay hands, he may receive the Holy Ghost. (Acts 8:15–19)

I don't see how it could get any clearer than that. So why all of the confusion among other churches?

There is a difference in having the influence of the Holy Ghost and in receiving the gift of the Holy Ghost. Under the influence of the Spirit, anyone can know the truth of all things if they ask God, the Father, with a sincere heart.

Through the following scriptural passage, I have come to an important realization.

> When Jesus came into the coasts of Caesarea Philippi, he asked his disciples, saying, Whom do men say that I the Son of man am?
>
> And they said, Some say that thou art John the Baptist: some, Elias; and others, Jeremias, or one of the prophets.
>
> He saith unto them, But whom say ye that I am?
>
> And Simon Peter answered and said, Thou art the Christ, the Son of the living God.
>
> And Jesus answered and said unto him, Blessed art thou, Simon Bar-jona: for flesh and blood hath not revealed it unto thee, but my Father which is in heaven.
>
> And I say also unto thee, That thou art Peter, and upon this rock I will build my church; and the gates of hell shall not prevail against it.
>
> And I will give unto thee the keys of the kingdom of heaven: and whatsoever thou shalt bind on earth shall be bound in heaven: and whatsoever thou shalt loose on earth shall be loosed in heaven.

> Then charged he his disciples that they should tell no man that he was Jesus the Christ. (Matthew 16:13–20)

At this point in the scriptures, the Comforter (the Holy Ghost) had not been given to anyone on earth because Jesus was still walking among men. In other words, the gift of the Holy Ghost was not available yet.

However, though the gift of the Holy Ghost wasn't possible yet, His influence *was* available. I believe this is how Heavenly Father revealed who Christ was to Peter. Let's take another look at verse 17 in this passage: "And Jesus answered and said unto him, Blessed art thou, Simon Bar-jona: for flesh and blood hath not revealed it unto thee, but my Father which is in heaven."

I believe this is how Heavenly Father reveals truth to us today, by the *influence* and power of the Holy Ghost.

There are many who do not join the LDS Church because they don't know how to discern between the *influence* and the *gift* of the Holy Ghost. If only they would kneel and pray to God, ask Him to reveal the truth to them, and humble themselves to receive it, He would give it to them. The Holy Ghost reveals truth to all who ask with a sincere heart and seek God diligently.

Having the gift of the Holy Ghost means we, through our obedience to God's commandments, have the Spirit of God present with us to lead us and guide us at all times and in all places. He, the Spirit, is our constant companion. Did your hear me? I said *constant* companion.

My "hallelujah" moment came when I realized I had this great companion to lead and guide me in all things and to reveal all truth to me. This is an amazing gift from our Father in Heaven.

We humans tend to make our paths through this life more difficult than they need to be. Think about it. God gave us a Savior who paid the price for our sins. Without this, it would be impossible to return to the Father's presence. On top of that, He's made the Holy Ghost available to us to act as a guide and testifier so that we're not fooled by the devil's crafty lies and so that we can stay on the straight and narrow path.

This doesn't mean the path won't be difficult or that the challenges we face won't push us to our limits. But it does mean that no matter the challenge, God is with us and will help us through. Elder David B. Haight, an apostle who has since passed on, once said, "The Lord never asks the impossible. Often the difficult, but never the impossible."

Our Heavenly Father really did think of everything to help bring us back into His presence.

I MENTIONED EARLIER that I love charity. Let me share with you what the Holy Ghost has taught me about charity.

I've read 1 Corinthians 13 many times throughout my life. In fact, I've memorized the entire chapter—all thirteen verses! Not until a few years ago did I have a desire to pray and ask God what this chapter is all about.

I often wondered how anyone could do the things mentioned in this chapter and *not* have charity. I thought all the deeds and characteristics contained in that chapter were what charity is all about.

One day, however, I got on my knees and asked my Father what charity really is. Sometimes when we think we've got it, we don't, and when we think we are, we ain't! Pride keeps us off of our knees and keeps us from seeking God in spirit and truth. This is why so many are lost, following after man's understanding. They're looking for love in all the wrong places!

So, if charity isn't all the things mentioned in 1 Corinthians 13, then what is God's definition of charity? I understood it to be the list of qualities listed in verses 4–8.

> Charity suffereth long, and is kind; charity envieth not; charity vaunteth not itself, is not puffed up,
> Doth not behave itself unseemly, seeketh not her own, is not easily provoked, thinketh no evil;
> Rejoiceth not in iniquity, but rejoiceth in the truth;
> Beareth all things, believeth all things, hopeth all things, endureth all things.

Charity never faileth: but whether there be prophecies, they shall fail; whether there be tongues, they shall cease; whether there be knowledge, it shall vanish away.

After I asked with a sincere heart through prayer, this is what my Father revealed to me about charity: charity is not the act itself but the spirit upon which the act or deed travels.

Let that thought sink into your heart and marinate for a minute.

Think about this. Words alone won't hurt you; it's the spirit with which those words travel that *can* hurt you. Flesh and blood did not reveal this to me, but my Father in Heaven.

When we don't receive the gift of the Holy Ghost, or we don't do the things required of us to have the Spirit with us always, we're missing out on one of God's greatest gifts. When I don't have the Holy Ghost with me, it feels like I'm in a dark room, groping to find my way.

For way too many years, I underappreciated the gift of the Holy Ghost that I'd received after baptism by the proper authority into the LDS Church. I lived well below my spiritual potential, simply because I didn't seek my Father's spiritual guidance through the holy gift He'd given me.

As I mentioned earlier, I had no desire to receive the priesthood and its inherent responsibilities after joining the Church. I also had no desire to go to the temple or receive any of the blessings that come from going there. I leaned instead on my own understanding and thought that what I had was good enough. My heart was in the wrong place. I'd stopped asking the right questions in a continuing quest for learning the truth of all things.

Behold, I would exhort you that when ye shall read these things, if it be wisdom in God that ye should read them, that ye would remember how merciful the Lord hath been unto the children of men, from the creation of Adam even down until the time that ye shall receive these things, and ponder it in your hearts.

And when ye shall receive these things, I would exhort you that ye would ask God, the Eternal Father, in the name of Christ, if these things are not true; and if ye shall ask with a sincere heart, with real intent, having faith in Christ, he will manifest the truth of it unto you, by the power of the Holy Ghost.

And by the power of the Holy Ghost ye may know the truth of all things. (Moroni 10:3–5)

There you have it. Ask God with a sincere heart, with real intent, and with faith in Christ, and He will reveal the truth of all things by the power of the Holy Ghost.

Hallelujah! It feels wonderful to be in love under new management!

CHAPTER 16

DO YOU HEAR YO MAMA CALLIN' YOU?

"DISCIPLINE IS NOT the enemy of enthusiasm." This line is from the movie *Lean on Me*, starring Morgan Freeman as the main character, Joe Clark. This is one of my favorite movie quotes, especially as it relates to raising a family.

Sebrina and I have raised seven children—six boys and one girl. When it comes to raising six boys, no quote rings truer to my ears than this one. Many have asked how we've raised seven good kids, and to be honest, we owe any success we've had as parents to our faith in and testimony of the gospel of Jesus Christ.

We've come to realize that effective parenting requires communication. I knew that when Sebrina and I got married, we needed to be on the same page when it came to raising our children. One of the first questions I asked Sebrina while we were seriously dating was what her views were on disciplining our children. I also wanted to know how she felt about me disciplining her children, the ones she'd had from her first marriage. Exploring these questions brought us to an understanding and agreement that in our home there would be no "yours, mine, and ours" children. We wanted one big, happy family, and the only steps (as in stepchildren) would be the ones leading from our house's lower level to its upper level.

That's how all the kids became *our* kids. Our exes didn't like it, but not liking what we did is how they became exes in the first place!

Sebrina and I were not going to allow anyone on the outside looking in to run our home, especially our exes. Once Sebrina and

I got married, the first thing we did was set ground rules for our former spouses. When her ex called, she let him know he had to deal with me and gave me the phone. When my ex called, I let her know she had to deal with my wife and handed the phone to Sebrina. It was difficult in the beginning. Our exes felt that because they were the biological parents, they had a say in what happened with the kids in *our* home. We cut that nonsense out real quick!

Sebrina's ex had all the access to the kids he wanted, but in his house, not ours! We never stopped him from coming to get the kids, but when the kids were with us, our word was law. We soon learned from his visits that Sebrina's ex not only wanted access to the kids but also wanted access to her. We cut that nonsense out too. When we stuck to our decision, he chose to fade away.

Consistency, our love for each other, and our love for the gospel of Jesus Christ are what helped us through this difficult transition.

Things with my ex, however, were a little different. In the beginning of my and Sebrina's marriage, my ex-wife had custody of the children we had in common. When my ex called and I handed the phone to Sebrina, it was like pulling teeth. My ex wasn't having it—or so she thought. Sebrina and I had prayerfully made a plan, and we stuck to it. When my ex no longer had free access to me, my life came into focus and I could keep my priorities straight. Sebrina played a huge role in that area of my life, and with Heavenly Father's help, she brought sanity into my life in regard to my ex.

Eventually, our exes understood that Sebrina and I were serious and we refused to let them have the access to us they wanted. As this became clearer to them, they eventually took their proper places. With these boundaries in place, we were able to focus all of our energy on raising our family with the gospel of Jesus Christ as our focal point.

At this time in our marriage, we only had each other, our church, and our family. Both of our parents had problems with the LDS Church and our marriage. Eventually, Sebrina's parents came around, but to this day, my mother is still opposed to our marriage and our religion.

Even without my mom onboard, we were in good company.

ONCE WE HAD things with our exes under control, we embarked on raising our kids the way we saw fit and in accordance with what the Lord's true Church taught.

Like any married couple, Sebrina and I had different ways of doing things in the beginning. On the one hand, I was used to changing diapers, cleaning, cooking, caring for the children, and having a full-time job. On the other hand, Sebrina didn't appreciate my hands-on style; she had her own idea of what our roles should be. I was the man, and she was the woman. She took care of the babies, the cooking, the cleaning, and all the other domestic things that needed to be done. My role was to go to work and provide. I didn't like this approach at all.

I recall once when I was about to change one of our kids' diapers, Sebrina was all like, "What are you doing?"

"Changing the baby's diaper."

"I'll do it!" she said and took the baby from me.

"Hey, I got it."

That didn't work, and she proceeded to change the baby like I wasn't even there. I was heated, to say the least.

Another disagreement came when I was cleaning our newborn's runny nose.

"What are you doing to my baby?" she asked.

"I'm cleaning his nose. What does it look like I'm doing?"

Once again, she took our baby from me as if I had no idea what I was doing. We discussed "my way" versus "her way" for the next three hours.

After several months of trying to prove to Sebrina that I was a better mother than she was, something hit me. *Wait a minute!* I thought. *I don't have to get up in the middle of the night and fix bottles anymore. I don't have to change dirty diapers anymore! All I have to do is go to work, play with the kids, and teach them things from time to time. Sebrina will take care of the rest! Why am I fighting this?*

This was an amazing deal. As soon as I let these thoughts sink into my thick skull, I realized it was time for me to stand up and be the man, father, husband, and son God created me to be.

I can't think of a better woman, mother, wife, or daughter of God than my Sebrina. My Father told me on that bus all those years ago to tell her she had a beautiful spirit, and He knew what He was talking about. Under the guidance of our Father, Sebrina has taken the broken and tattered man that I was and has restored me to a condition that is better than I have ever found myself in before. She helped me find the courage to believe in myself as a man, husband, and father.

I think of the Japanese word *kintsukuroi* when I consider what Sebrina and my Savior have done to help me become a better man. *Kintsukuroi* is a Japanese art technique in which broken ceramics are mended using gold and silver powders. It's an intensive process that is not easy to do and requires a lot of skill. When the broken item is fixed, however, it's adorned with veins of precious metal and is more beautiful than it was in its original form.

I was their broken ceramic, and now I am more beautiful than I was before! Because of this, I was ready to do my part in helping raise *our* children.

So how *did* we raise our kids to be kind, loving, well-mannered, and respectful people? We first had to work on fixing ourselves with the help of the Lord and let Him make us the parents we needed to be. Our greatest desire was to be good parents to our children, so we prayed together and asked God to bless us accordingly. Then we followed His perfect instructions.

On one occasion, we were traveling to Virginia with the kids and stopped to get something to eat. We got high chairs for the babies, and the other kids were big enough to sit at the table without booster chairs. After our food was served, we blessed it as we would at our dining room table at home. About halfway into our meal, an elderly couple came to our table as they were leaving, commented how nice it was to see a family praying, and asked us how we managed to get all our small children to pray and behave so well.

Sebrina smiled and said, "Practice." My wife, like she has been so many times, was right. Praying and behaving well weren't difficult for our family because it was what we practiced in our home every day. Folks still compliment us sometimes when we dine out, but this just illustrates how uncommon it is for people to address our Father in Heaven in public.

Sebrina and I tried to make sure that our kids understood that we were their parents, not their friends. We never had to worry about our kids acting out in sacrament meeting or in the grocery store, because we taught them how to behave at home. If Sebrina called one of the kids and they didn't respond in *my* time frame, I gave them "the look" and barked, "Do you hear yo mama callin' you?" Times like this are when the quote from *Lean on Me* came in handy. "Discipline is not the enemy of enthusiasm."

My wife and I have always been on the same page when it comes to disciplining our children. In order for discipline to work, we've learned that both of us have to be in agreement. We've tried all kinds of discipline when teaching our kids and have had a lot of trial and error along the way.

We've learned the hard way that reprimands should always be made with love and affection and that they have to be done consistently. If we deem a reprimand necessary for a specific behavior today, we *have* to deem it worthy of another reprimand the next time it comes around. The minute we get too tired to deal with the bad behavior and fail to reprimand again, all the hard work we did goes down the drain. Frustration sets in and we have to start back at square one.

There are so many ways to discipline a child that involve the pure love of Christ. We just have to be willing to love our children enough to pray and find out how. This is what Sebrina and I have strived to do for our children, and it seems to be working. Four of our children are adults now, and each of them is a beautiful contribution to society.

There's no guarantee our kids will grow into the men or women we want them to be because they sill have their agency to do with their lives what they will. They will still experience failures and successes, will win some and lose some. They will be better people because of the time we take to set them on the right course.

I've learned so much about God and His nature by being a father. I know He has a plan for each one of us and His plan is perfect and available to us through the teachings of the Church.

CHAPTER 17

KEEPIN' IT REAL

SINCE I'VE BEEN a member of the LDS Church, I've had many wonderful opportunities and experiences. My membership in the Church has helped me embrace our Heavenly Father's perfect plan, which is not being embraced by today's society as a whole. As hard as we might try to fight against it, the world's influences are finding their way into the Church. If we, Saints of the Most High, are distracted from the spiritual guidance the prophets offer and do not form personal and intimate relationships with our Heavenly Father and His Son, we might unwittingly help the ways of the world to infiltrate even further into the Church.

In a world dominated by political campaigns and ideological categories that do more to divide than unite, we as members of The Church of Jesus Christ of Latter-day Saints are often fighting for justice in an unjust world. We're fighting for equality in a society that supports and encourages separatism. It's easy for us to get caught up in the things of a temporary and fallen world while forgetting to maintain an eternal perspective. It's easy for us to expect our sufferings to be easy and our trials to be few. It's as if we've come to believe that we're entitled to justice and deserving of peace.

Sound doctrine, morals, and values are becoming extinct. Religion and societal norms have been divided and changed so as to meet man's will, not God's. There are so many worldly demands and responsibilities that compete for our time that the chasm between God's will and man's will is growing larger.

FROM BAPTIST PREACHER TO MORMON TEACHER

LDS Church leaders have counseled us repeatedly to read and study the scriptures, have regular family prayer, attend the temple and our church meetings, and so on. But what do we do when we follow this guidance and our lives and situations don't seem to get any better? This is when we stand and endure. This is when we seek our Father most sincerely and intently. This is when we change our perspectives.

It is better to be humble without being compelled to be humble. If we can do this, we will be better off when these times come because we will already be focused firmly on the eternal perspective. We will endure and stand in our place with the assurance that God is aware of us and will sustain us in our times of need.

Jesus taught that if we seek, we shall find. This lesson is as true today as it was two thousand years ago. We *will* find what we seek. If we want to find Heavenly Father's hand in all things, then we have to look for His hand in all things. If we want to spend our time in pursuit of what the world has to offer, we'll find that too!

However, we Latter-day Saints have an obligation to stay focused on eternal things. We should not take the sacred covenants we make with God when we're baptized, endowed, and sealed for granted.

In regard to our sacred responsibilities as husbands, wives, parents, and servants in Zion, we should do more than to just get by. Now is the time to strengthen our faith and build an unwavering testimony of our Savior, Jesus Christ, and His gospel. These are the times when the weak will fall and abandon their testimony. We have to be diligent and work hard not to be one of them.

The contentious environment of the world is pressuring us to choose a side. The mental, emotional, and physical stresses that we face in our daily lives can help the evil one sell us the lies and perspectives he hopes will destroy our eternal perspective. These views are being deviously introduced and accepted by many of God's children—including some of our own!

The problem with choosing sides is that the most important side has been strategically left out. God is slowly being asked to leave the stage while the ways of the world hog the spotlight. And it's all a setup!

Because many of us have different views on politics and society, the side we choose will be based on those perceptions. In light of all the different points of view and opinions, we as a society are losing sight of the Savior's words, "By this shall all men know that ye are my disciples, if ye have love one to another" (John 13:35). Love is the key ingredient in how God's children, no matter our race or religion, should treat each other.

Aside from us not showing enough love for one another, there are plenty of other things that are keeping us from reaching our divine potential. Many of us have become focused on the dangers of the world and give our attention to things that divert us from our Father's plan. We spend more time on social media expressing our frustrations and views and watching mindless cat videos than we do studying and teaching the good news of the gospel of Jesus Christ and serving as He would serve. The Lord did, after all, tell us to *feed* His sheep, not *Tweet* them!

I'll say it again. It's a setup!

Satan has led many hearts and minds to focus on what's wrong in the world instead of what's right. He knows that God's plan of salvation is what's most right with the world, which is why he's inciting so many to fight against it and anything associated with it—the Church included. The ills of today's world are nothing new; they just scream at us more loudly because of the widespread use of social media and the overabundance of TV and Internet media outlets.

The key to survival in these last days is to stand firm with our Church leaders. Hold fast to what they teach and counsel. If Jesus wants something to change in His Church, He'll let His prophets know. We need to stand united if we are to weather the storms of the latter days. "Now I beseech you, brethren, by the name of our Lord Jesus Christ, that ye all speak the same thing, and that there be no divisions among you; but that ye be perfectly joined together in the same mind and in the same judgment" (1 Corinthians 1:10).

Yes, the battle is real. The suffering and trials are hard. But we should not be surprised, nor should we be afraid. We should stand as one body and dwell in one mind, firmly united in the faith of our Savior Jesus Christ. These are the perilous times the scriptures have warned us about. We should stand united with no divisions among us. Black, white, bond, and free, "all are alike unto God" (2 Nephi 26:33).

The only division that should exist is the division between what's right and what's wrong. How do we know the difference? The same way we gained our testimonies about the gospel in the first place: pray about it. The Spirit will never lead us astray. As we live worthily and keep our heart and mind pure, He will whisper to us, ever so sweetly, about what is right and true.

CHAPTER 18

LET THERE BE LIGHT

I N 2003, A pair of sister missionaries told Sebrina and me about a Church auxiliary named The Genesis Group. We'd never heard of the group before and were further interested when the sisters told us it was a group designed specifically to help with African American LDS Church member retention and to help them transition into the LDS culture. It was like a dream come true. My wife and I were instantly excited about the prospect of such a group and wanted to learn more.

The Genesis Group is an auxiliary of The Church of Jesus Christ of Latter-day Saints that is intended to help black Church members support each other with fellowship and love. Since most black LDS were the only members of African descent in their local wards and stakes, the Church realized that these members had unique issues and would benefit from associating with each other. The group was created in 1971 under the direction of then-junior Apostles Gordon B. Hinckley, Thomas S. Monson, and Boyd K. Packer. Ruffin Bridgeforth led the group from its inception until his passing in 1997. Darius Gray led the group from 1997 to 2003, and Don Harwell has led the group since 2003. Elder David T. Warner, Area Seventy, Fifth Quorum, is the current Church area authority that oversees the group. ("Genesis Group," *Wikipedia*, accessed 7 May 2015, http://en.wikipedia.org/wiki/Genesis_Group; "New Area Seventies Called to Fifth Quorum," *Church News*, accessed 15 May 2015, https://www.lds.org/church/news/new-area-seventies-called-to-fifth-quorum?lang=eng)

The Genesis Group was just what the doctor ordered. God is good—and all the time! Let the Church say *amen*!

We were disappointed to learn that at that time, the only Genesis Group was in Salt Lake City, so we had to figure out a way to start a group in Columbus, Ohio, where we were living then. I researched the group and sought counsel from my bishop, who took it to the stake president, who in turn counseled with a local presiding authority. In the end, local Church leadership determined that we could not start a group in our area. We were told that the Church leadership didn't want to start a church within a church. I was crushed, but not derailed.

I've learned in life that when people tell me no, what they really mean is *know*. I needed to be more specific in what it was I was asking for, and I needed to explain it in greater detail. So I took to the Internet to see if I could find anyone who was having the same issues. Later that year, I came across a black LDS brother in Los Angeles who also wanted to bring a Genesis group to Southern California. In fact, he'd been trying for longer than I had. He gave me a few ideas that I took back to my bishop, only to be told *know*.

Back to the drawing board.

About a year later, I was feeling discouraged because we were no closer to getting a Genesis Group in Ohio than we were when we first started. I'd come across many people who wanted a group in their stake, but to no avail. So, I decided to reach out to Don Harwell, who was—and still is—the Salt Lake City Genesis Group leader. Surprisingly, Don was going to be in Columbus on business and offered to meet with me. I was so excited about this that I told my bishop, who in turn asked me to invite Don to speak in our ward. Don accepted the invitation and delivered a powerful message in our ward's sacrament meeting.

My son Isaiah was twelve at the time and hadn't been baptized yet. We left the decision regarding baptism up to our sons, LeRoy Jr. and Isaiah, because they didn't live with us at the time. We were afraid that if they were pressured into baptism, they wouldn't have the support they needed.

Anyway, my son Isaiah felt the Spirit so strongly during Don's talk that he made a beeline to the podium after sacrament meeting to talk to him. Surprisingly, and unbeknownst to Sebrina and me, Isaiah asked Don if he would baptize him. Don escorted our son back to us and, with a surprised look on his face, told me what Isaiah had asked of him.

In the LDS faith, it's tradition for a father—if he's a worthy priesthood-holding member of the Church—to baptize his children. Don was well aware of this and didn't want to overstep his bounds, not to mention that he lived in Utah and a trip back to Ohio wasn't like a trip around the corner to the local 7-Eleven. I told Don I had no problem with him baptizing our son, if it was not too much of an inconvenience to him. Don returned a few weeks later and baptized Isaiah. It was a beautiful experience.

As you can see, while we couldn't reach out and touch Genesis, Genesis was able and more than willing to reach out to us and to bless our lives. But we weren't giving up on bringing a local chapter to Ohio. About two and a half years later, my contact in California had a brilliant idea: we could run an unofficial local Genesis Group, based on the Salt Lake City group, with no priesthood authority over it. Kind of like a book club, but minus the books. We would hold our meetings in various church meetinghouses, as long as the stake president agreed.

Uh-oh, I thought, *here we go again.*

I took the proposal to my bishop, and he took it to the stake president. After nearly three years of trying, the stake president agreed to let us start a local Genesis chapter! So in 2006, we held our first Genesis group meeting in the stake center adjacent to the Columbus Ohio Temple. Our guest speaker was Darius Gray, who led the Genesis Group in Salt Lake 1997–2003, and that stake center was packed to overflowing that night!

Like the Salt Lake group, we held our meetings on the first Sunday of each month. Our group attendance grew with each meeting, and word about the Ohio group's success was shared on several occasions in the Salt Lake group's newsletter. We felt very blessed at this time.

Then it all came tumbling down.

I received a job offer in Virginia. It was an offer I couldn't refuse, so we moved shortly afterward. When we arrived in Chesapeake,

Virginia, all I wanted to do in regards to Church was attend my meetings and nothing else. I'd spent three years working hard to bring a Genesis chapter to Ohio. I didn't want any part in trying to do the same for Virginia. Sebrina and I didn't say a word to each other about Genesis.

Our first stake conference in our new stake was a surprise to us. Not that anything apostate was taught from the pulpit, or anything like that. What surprised us was that the stake president made his way directly to us after the meeting to talk to us. We introduced ourselves, and we made small talk for a minute or two before the president lowered the boom.

"Have either of you ever heard of The Genesis Group?" I lowered my head in silent laughter and looked at my wife as she gave me that smile that only she can give.

"Why, yes, President, we have. In fact, we helped start a chapter in the stake we just move from!"

"Really?" the president responded. "I've been praying that we would find someone to help start a Genesis Group here! How would you feel about starting one here?

I won't bore you with the details behind that endeavor, but I will tell you that it was a lot easier to do in Virginia than it was in Ohio. We held our first meeting in the stake president's home a few months later.

Then, like before, a change in plans came along. The company I was working as a loan officer for went under in 2008, and I lost my job. I found another, but in Terre Haute, Indiana. *Will someone get U-Haul on the line—again?*

Once again, we had no desire to start a Genesis Group in Indiana, and for the next five years, we went into Genesis hiding. Our bishop had become a close family friend during our time in Indiana, and to our surprise, he talked to us about possibly starting a group. But Indiana was different for us, and the Lord needed us in a different way. While serving on the high council there, I got a prompting I never expected to receive, especially because I'd told my family we'd never do what I was being guided to do. *Someone get U-Haul on the line again. We're moving to Utah!*

Eleven years after first hearing about the Genesis Group, I attended my first Salt Lake City Genesis Group meeting in September 2014. Don Harwell was still the president and was quite surprised to see me, as I hadn't told him about moving my family. He had me stand and introduce myself and then gave the group a brief rundown of my and Sebrina's efforts to bring the group to Ohio and Virginia.

Don and I embraced after the meeting and exchanged phone numbers. He called a few weeks later and told me the Lord wanted me to serve as the second counselor in the Genesis Group presidency. My heart hit the floor. I never expected such a calling. *Someone call the paramedics!* After I came to, I accepted the calling and have since come to realize that the Lord had blessed me once again. He'd led me to Utah so He could bless me even more for my efforts on His behalf. It's humbling to realize that I am part of only the third-ever Genesis Group leadership. My name is going to be associated with great men that have led the group in the past, such as Ruffin Bridgeforth, Darius Gray, Eugene Orr, Don Harwell, and Eddie Gist. I pray that my journey with Genesis will be as spiritually beneficial to others as these men's have been.

CHAPTER 19

CALLED TO SERVE

MY LIFE WAS changed through the service of LDS missionaries. Missionary work is something that has touched my life constantly since I first met the elders in Sebrina's apartment in the mid-1990s. I've been taught by missionaries, served with missionaries, had my own missionary experiences, and have loved every minute of them. In light of the love Sebrina and I have developed for missionary work over the years, it makes sense that one of our children became a missionary.

Male members of the LDS Church are encouraged to serve a two-year mission for the Church when they reach the age of eighteen. Some serve when they're a little older, and some don't serve at all. A mission is *strongly encouraged*, but not *required*. Though it's not demanded of them, many young LDS men choose to give up two years of their lives to preach the gospel of Jesus Christ anyway. While on missions, these young men share their faith and the Church's teachings with those who are not members of our church and who are willing to listen. Our missionaries also spend time working with people who once embraced the Church but have since stopped associating with the Church and its members, for whatever reason. Young women are also welcomed to serve an eighteen-month mission, but at the age of nineteen.

Personally, I think a mission is one of the best ways for young men to prepare for life. Missions teach young men—and women—lessons and skills that will serve them well throughout their lives.

Budgeting, time management, social skills, faith-promoting experiences, and leadership opportunities are but a few of the lessons and skills missionaries gain while serving a mission. Who wouldn't benefit from developing those types of skills and having these types of experiences?

Our son Isaiah was the first of our children to serve a full-time mission—but it didn't look like he would at first. Isaiah has always loved football. From playing peewee football to watching the pros of the National Football League, my boy loved all things pertaining to the gridiron. So, it came as no surprise to us when he chose to go to college and play football instead of serving a mission. Sebrina and I had hoped he'd serve a mission, but we always left these types of decisions entirely up to our children. We knew how important it was for our sons to enter manhood by building a solid foundation—and a mission would do that very thing for him—but we were not about to force him to go. We knew that a mission is part of our Heavenly Father's perfect plan for His sons, but we also remembered whose plan it was to force obedience—and we wanted no part of that nonsense!

It was obvious Isaiah had other plans, which included playing football on a partial scholarship at Grand Rapids Community College in Grand Rapids, Michigan.

Dropping my son off at college was not an easy task. I lingered around the campus for as long as I could, trying to avoid the inevitable good-bye. Once he was settled into his apartment, he asked me to drop him off at the football field so he could get right to work. That's Isaiah for you; he doesn't believe in wasting time.

I took him to the football field where several of his teammates were already there working out. He introduced me, and we took some pictures, and then I hugged my son, kissed him good-bye, and drove away. I cried like a baby as I watched my son grow smaller in my rearview mirror. Don't let anyone know about that part, okay?

Isaiah wound up redshirting that season and, six months later, called me in the middle of the night to tell me the Lord had called him to serve a mission and that he wanted to come home right away to prepare. A few days later, I was headed back to Michigan to pick up my son.

ISAIAH MET WITH the bishop as soon as we got home, but the mission preparation phase wasn't all that easy at first. Isaiah had some things he had to work through before he could be fully ready, so Sebrina and I gave all the support we could.

About a year later, Isaiah submitted his paperwork and received his official mission call to serve in the Louisiana Baton Rouge Mission. We were excited, as are most LDS folks whose children serve missions. He'd worked so hard to prepare, and now all his hard work had paid off.

We role-played a lot to help Isaiah prepare for his mission. I taught him some of the techniques I'd learned during my career as a salesman, which proved to be helpful for him on his mission. On December 18, 2012, we loaded the family into our van and took Isaiah to the airport in Indianapolis to fly to the missionary training center in Provo, Utah. You'll remember from a previous chapter that my missionary picked Isaiah up at the Salt Lake City Airport and took him to the MTC. I still love recalling that tender mercy!

After all the trials Isaiah went through to get ready, he was finally on his mission. My wife and I smiled and gave each other the "We did it!" look. I thought the hard part was over, but boy, was I wrong! I figured the blessings would start rolling in. And they did, just not in the ways I expected.

HAVE YOU EVER missed a blessing because it didn't come in the package you thought it would or should? Because of my personal expectations, I've overlooked many blessings this way. My wife, bless her heart, saw the blessings from our son serving a mission right from the start. I, as usual, took a little longer to see what she'd seen all along. I expected the blessings to come in the form of George Washingtons, Abraham Lincolns, and lots of Andrew Jacksons! I expected our financial needs to not only be met, but figured our money cup would run over!

Well, the blessings didn't roll in the way I thought they would. The true blessings came as the Lord helped us navigate our trials with strength and patience. We made it through our challenges and gained priceless wisdom and knowledge along the way. Our testimonies grew by leaps and bounds! Our love for each other and the gospel of Jesus Christ was stronger than ever before. *All is well, all is well!* Or was it?

Isaiah's grandmother passed away while he was on his mission, and it was difficult for him to deal with the loss because he was very close to her. His mission president even called us looking for direction and advice on how to help our son deal with his grandmother's passing. Isaiah wanted to come home, but after talking with us on the phone, he found the strength to stay in the mission field. Something we said got through to him, because that boy put his nose to the grind after that and never looked back.

Isaiah's two years passed quickly. I promised him before he left that we'd pick him up from his mission when he was done. We lived in Indiana at the time, and I had no idea we'd be living in Utah when it came time to deliver. Those money blessings I hoped for when Isaiah left on his mission? Well, they started rolling in when we needed them most to go pick our boy up in Louisiana. Not large amounts of cash, but more than we needed to make the 72-hour round trip by car. A family in Isaiah's mission—the Tolberts—was gracious enough to host and feed us while we were in town. And let me tell you—the food was off the chizzle! (That means really good.) We also met a lot of people who had fallen in love with our missionary while he served in Louisiana.

Isaiah had become so focused on the Lord's work that it blew my mind. One morning while we were there, I'd gotten up early, and to my surprise, I found Isaiah on his knees in prayer before anyone in the house was awake. Not wanting to disturb him, I stood in the doorway for several minutes watching my son pray, feeling so happy and blessed that he'd learned the importance of keeping in touch with his Heavenly Father.

EVENTUALLY, IT WAS time to go home, but we had one item of business left to take care of before we hit the road. The local Church unit had put together a fireside to see Isaiah off and asked Sebrina and me to speak. It was an amazing meeting! So many members and investigators showed up to express their love and to see our missionary off on his next adventure. The Spirit was strong in that meeting, and it took us a while to leave afterward because people just kept coming and coming to say good-bye to Elder Myers.

While on the road, Isaiah realized that he was now headed "home" to a home he'd never seen before, and that was 1,400 miles from the home he knew in Terre Haute. All the friends and families he'd known and loved in Indiana were nothing but a memory. He was going to have to start all over, and it was tough for him at first. But with Heavenly Father on our side, nothing is impossible. It's been a difficult transition, but one that's well worth the effort and sacrifice.

CHAPTER 20

STEADFAST AND FIRM

WHEN I WAS a child, every time my family moved, my mother had us all kneel in prayer while she asked God for a special blessing on our new home. In those prayers, she asked Him to post an angel at each of the four corners of our new home so we would be protected from the north, south, east, and west. We always felt better after my mother prayed over our home. We lived in some ghettos, but we were never robbed and nobody ever did us physical harm.

I've taken to following my mom's example in every home I've lived in since. As a member of the LDS Church armed with the holy priesthood, I've followed my mom's example and asked that my Father post angels at the four corners of each house we've lived in to protect us from the north, south, east, and west. We've been kept safe from burglary and physical harm in every home we've lived.

Experiences like this have contributed greatly to the faith that sustains me today. As my faith has grown, I've learned to exercise it consistently. Faith works when we exercise it! Faith is how we protect our family, and ourselves, from the fiery darts of the adversary.

Since joining the Church in 1995, my testimony and faith have grown more than at any time in my life. My faith and testimony have grown because, like all of ours, they've been tried and tested. Nonmembers often ask me how I know the LDS Church is true. It's simple, actually. God told me!

The scriptures teach us that faith is the substance of things hoped for and the evidence of things not seen. Faith comes by hearing and reading the word of God and then applying it to our lives. If we want our testimony to grow and become solid, we must walk by faith, not by sight.

When people tell me that they've asked God if the LDS Church is true and haven't received an answer, I know that they aren't truly relying on God for the answer. Instead, they're relying on their own understanding for the answer.

Questions like "Why did the Mormons practice polygamy?" and "If the Church is true, why did they withhold the priesthood from black men for so long?" keep them from understanding and receiving God's answer, which will only come from the Holy Ghost to an honest heart.

A young man once said to me, "Wain, I don't get it. There are so many issues and past practices with the LDS Church that are bothersome." I responded by pointing out that his issues with the Church are all based on the actions of man, not God. I've dealt with—and continue to deal with—the problems I have because my faith is in God, not man. Members of the LDS Church are human and have shortcomings and flaws, just like everyone else. I can't judge them; I've got too many of my own weaknesses and sins to correct.

"So why does the Church have prophets if you're not supposed to put your trust in man?" he continued.

Simple, I told him. God leads His Church *through* prophets. He leads families *through* each family's patriarch. He leads individuals *through* personal revelation. The formula is simple, beautiful, and leads down a straight and narrow path back to our Heavenly Father. Personal revelation should be in accordance with the family patriarch's. The patriarch's leadership should line up with the prophet's. The prophet's instructions and counsel will align with God's instructions. If followed by faith, the formula is perfect. It's man and his many faults that complicate the process.

For example, there are some televangelists today that are big into preaching about prosperity and that God wants us to be prosperous. God wanting us to prosper makes sense, but many interpret this as God not wanting us to be poor. So what happens then? Man puts

God into a formula that makes sense to him. If a televangelist's congregation follows his instructions, they'll put their money into the preacher's ministry. When do this, the preacher says, God will bless them with wealth like He's blessed the preacher. The preacher would have the donator believe that once they do this, they will be wealthy, righteous, happy, and well on their way to heaven.

I understand the mindset that God doesn't want me to be poor, but in Romans 8:28, we're told that for those who love God, all things will work together for their good. In my life, I've learned to trust the Lord and have seen those words fulfilled.

IN THIS BOOK, I've shared some of the experiences I've had on the path from being a Baptist preacher to becoming a Mormon teacher. Each step of the way that's led forward, I've relied on my faith, which is such an important part of drawing nearer to God and His Only Begotten Son.

I used to think the scripture that teaches if we can just have faith that's as a grain of a mustard seed, then we can do miracles. For many years, I understood this comparison to mean that faith was about size. One day, it dawned on me that there are seeds smaller than a mustard seed. So why didn't Jesus compare faith to a seed that's smaller than a mustard seed?

I researched this and learned that a mustard seed is so strong that it can grow just about anywhere. So, He wasn't talking about the *size* of the mustard seed; He was referring to the *strength* of the mustard seed and the fact that it, like our faith, can grow anywhere.

By hearing and reading the words of God and then opening our hearts to them, faith can take root and grow within us no matter where we are and no matter what life brings our way. When all is said and done, my testimony of The Church of Jesus Christ of Latter-day Saints is founded in this simple truth: I know it's true because God told me it's true.

James 1:5, the same scripture that sent Joseph Smith into the woods to ask God which church he should join, says that if *any* person—not just prophets, His chosen servants, or the righteous—wants to ask Him a question, that person is more than welcome to ask Him! Since any man can ask, I decided to ask and learned for myself.

This is how I came to know that the LDS Church is true. He'll tell you the same if you honestly ask with an open mind and heart and are willing to accept His answer. It's a simple formula that will lead to an eternity of happiness.

What are you waiting for? Go ask Him!

Already asked Him and know it's true? Ask Him again. He's happy to tell you again.

ABOUT WAIN MYERS

WAIN MYERS IS a native of Dayton, Ohio, and a graduate of John H. Patterson High School, where he was a state discus champion and musician. After graduation, Wain enlisted in the United States Army and served a tour of duty in Bad Kissingen, Germany. There he received his call to the ministry. After his military career, Wain returned to the US and began preaching at True Vine Missionary Baptist Church. He preached for over five years and was then introduced to the LDS Church by his lovely now-wife, Sebrina.

Wain developed a passion for finance after his military career and enrolled in the Alpha & Omega College of Real Estate in Virginia Beach, Virginia, and became a loan originator in 2007. Investing in his insurance business, he and his family moved to Terre Haut, Indiana, in 2009. Wain became active in the Terre Haute community in such activities as ambassador in the Terre Haute Chamber of Commerce, Terre Haute Symphony board member, member of Terre Haute Young Leaders, and a proud "Big" of the Vigo County Big Brother Big Sister program. He is also a member of the Terre Haute Masonic Lodge #19. Wain has been an active member in The Church of Jesus Christ of the Latter-day Saints since 1995 and served on the Bloomington Indiana Stake High Council before moving to Salt Lake City, Utah, and being call as second counselor in the Genesis Group presidency.

Wain and Sebrina are the proud parents of seven amazing children: LeRoy Jr.; Isaiah; Bradford and his wife, Paige; Quesley; Braxton; Spencer; and Ammon. Wain is a firm believer that "when obedience ceases to be an irritant and becomes our quest, in that moment God will endow us with power" (Ezra Taft Benson, quoted in Donald L. Staheli, "Obedience—Life's Great Challenge," *Ensign*, May 1998, 82).

ABOUT KELLY L. MARTINEZ

KELLY L. MARTINEZ is a seasoned journalist whose work has appeared in a variety of publications, including *USA Today*, the *Los Angeles Times*, *Meridian* Magazine, and the *Deseret News*. He holds a bachelor's degree in communication and history from Utah Valley University and hails from southern California. He's worked in a variety of marketing and graphic design positions for more than twenty years. Of all his past work experience, he considers his four-season stint as a member of the Los Angeles Clippers' game-night stat crew to be his most enjoyable. Martinez and his wife are the parents of three adult sons, a daughter-in-law, and a preteen daughter who is growing up way too quickly. This is his first coauthorship and published book, but he did contribute an essay to *Famous Family Nights*, which was published by Cedar Fort in 2009. He and his family live in northern Utah.

SCAN TO VISIT

WWW.AUTHORWAINMYERS.COM